Praise for *Exceptional Customer Service*

With few exceptions, the typical retail experience is little more than a disappointment . . . The question is, do companies really understand what it takes to create exceptional customer service? Lisa Ford, David McNair, and Bill Perry provide the wisdom and tools essential for companies to build that phenomenal experience every customer yearns for. Great learning, especially important in these tough economic times when every detail matters.

Mike Tattersfield
President and CEO
Caribou Coffee Company

The City of Charleston, South Carolina, was cited in 2008 by *Travel and Leisure* as the friendliest in the U.S., and for eleven years our city has been named the "Most Mannerly" in the country. We have used the information in this wonderful book to guide all facets of our city staff to new heights of customer service excellence.

Joseph P. Riley, Jr.
Mayor
City of Charleston, SC

If anyone ever asks "Who wrote THE book on customer service?"—this is it. Lisa Ford, David McNair, and Bill Perry absolutely nail the keys to winning and keeping customers. Now more than ever, customer loyalty has to be a top priority for any business. If you want to create truly compelling experiences for your customers then get this book for everyone on your team.

Joe Calloway
Author, *Becoming a Category of One*

Praise for *Exceptional Customer Service*

In this practical and engaging book, Lisa Ford, David McNair, and Bill Perry provide the what, why, and how of world class service. Read it and you'll find out why their work and speeches have helped so many organizations take their service to new levels.

Mark Sanborn
Speaker, author of *The Fred Factor* and *You Don't Need a Title*

At Goodwill Industries, providing exceptional customer service to our patrons and donors provides the resources to fulfill our mission of eliminating barriers to opportunity and helping people in need reach their fullest potential through the power of work. Over 20,000 employees of Goodwill Industries nationwide have used the material in this outstanding book to help brand service excellence in their retail stores and donation centers.

George Kessenger
Former President and CEO
Goodwill Industries International

Anyone thinking about writing another book about customer service can turn off their computer and put down their pen. The perfect customer service book has now been written. *Exceptional Customer Service* doesn't just describe what good customer service is, it provides examples and exercises that allow anyone to make these concepts second nature. This book is a "must-read" for everyone who has to interact with people.

Michael Swartz
Senior Vice President, Administrative Services
Standard Parking Corporation

2ND EDITION

EXCEPTIONAL CUSTOMER SERVICE

2ND EDITION

EXCEPTIONAL CUSTOMER SERVICE

EXCEED CUSTOMER EXPECTATIONS TO BUILD LOYALTY & BOOST PROFITS

LISA FORD, DAVID McNAIR, AND WILLIAM PERRY

FOREWORD BY TONY HSIEH, CEO OF ZAPPOS.COM

BUSINESS

AVON, MASSACHUSETTS

Published by Adams Business, an imprint of
Adams Media, a division of F+W Media, Inc.
57 Littlefield Street, Avon, MA 02322. U.S.A.
www.adamsmedia.com

ISBN 10: 1-60550-038-0
ISBN 13: 978-1-60550-038-6

Printed in the United States of America.

J I H G F E D C B A

Library of Congress Cataloging-in-Publication Data
is available from the publisher.

This publication is designed to provide accurate and authoritative information
with regard to the subject matter covered. It is sold with the understanding that
the publisher is not engaged in rendering legal, accounting, or other professional
advice. If legal advice or other expert assistance is required, the services of a competent professional person should be sought.

—From a *Declaration of Principles* jointly adopted by a Committee of the
American Bar Association and a Committee of Publishers and Associations

Many of the designations used by manufacturers and sellers to distinguish their
product are claimed as trademarks. Where those designations appear in this book
and Adams Media was aware of a trademark claim, the designations have been
printed with initial capital letters.

"Bullseye" cartoons copyright © McNair/Nation.

This book is available at quantity discounts for bulk purchases.
For information, please call 1-800-289-0963.

A Special Note of Thanks!

Each of us owes a great deal of thanks to our incredibly supportive families for their love and patience with us as we've constructed this book. Our spouses, children (and for Bill—grandchildren), parents, and other extended family members have endured our constant and sometimes vigilant focus on service in everyday life. It's a 24/7 experiential relationship and one never can "leave it at the office." With all our love, L, D, and B.

Contents

Foreword to Second Edition

I'm always excited whenever I learn about a book devoted to delivering exceptional customer service, so I'm honored to be writing the foreword to a book with *Exceptional Customer Service* as the actual title.

At Zappos.com, our long-term vision is for the Zappos brand to be about the very best customer service and the very best customer experience. We sell a lot of different items today, including shoes, clothing, and bags, and we have customer-friendly policies such as free shipping both ways and a 365-day return policy.

But you may be surprised to learn that our number-one priority is actually not customer service. It's company culture. Our belief is that if you get the culture right, then most of the other stuff, like great customer service or building a great brand, will happen naturally on its own.

I'm reminded of a story in which one of our Customer Loyalty (call center) representatives answered the phone and was surprised to hear from a customer from Santa Monica, California, in the middle of the night. The customer said she was really, really hungry and would really like to order a pizza. While it's true we do sell a variety of items at Zappos, we don't actually sell pizza. At least not yet.

The customer explained that she was stuck in a hotel in the middle of the night and that room service had stopped serving hot food. She knew Zappos had great customer service and wanted to know what we could do to help.

Without missing a beat, the Zappos representative put the customer on hold and two minutes later came back with the list of the five closest places in Santa Monica that were still delivering pizza at that hour.

Clearly, this type of situation doesn't happen every day at Zappos. And truth be told, I was a little apprehensive about putting this story in this book, because I don't want Zappos to be flooded with phone calls from people trying to order pizza. But I think it's a fun story that illustrates the power of building a great service-focused culture. If you get the culture right, then even strange, unanticipated situations will be handled in a way that reflects positively on your company's brand.

Everyone knows that customer service is important, but most companies don't do it very well. Why is that?

It's because most companies are missing a culture made up of passionate, service-focused employees, and they're at a loss as to how to go about building it.

If you're wondering how to build a customer-focused culture, the book you're holding in your hands is a great starting point. This book isn't just about inspiring people to deliver great service. It's filled with plenty of exercises, tips, stories, and plans for bringing your culture to the next level.

It's never too late to start down the path of making your organization more customer-focused. The next step is easy. All you have to do is turn the page.

Tony Hsieh
CEO, Zappos.com

Foreword

How better to introduce you to this book than to tell you just why I like it. There's been much written about customer service through the years. Just look in the bookstores and Internet libraries, and see the vast materials available on customer service. That's not surprising when you consider that we, in the service profession, have been at this business of trying to please—better yet—to delight customers since the beginning of time.

Consider the phrase "customer service." We gloss over it in speaking and we print it on signs, in brochures, and in advertisements. How often do we stop and think of the profound implications of those two simple words? As for 'customer,' each of us walks in these shoes every day. You would think that alone makes us eminently qualified to evaluate, critique, and, hopefully, improve our own service delivery. Also, as customers we are better educated, have vastly greater access to information, and, most of all, have far more choices for buying goods and services than did our parents.

All of which makes the second word, 'service,' such a very important part of the phrase. All the research shows that today's consumer makes buying decisions based 10 percent on product and 90 percent on service. But, if you do not receive the service, the value of the product, then you did not get what you paid for. Enough said?

I am no stranger to customer service. Ritz-Carlton Hotels are often cited as one of the world's true icons of exceptional customer service. Of this, I am personally very proud. For our people, who serve so willingly and tirelessly, I am truly and deeply grateful. For this question that I am asked repeatedly, "How do you instill such a consistently high level of service?" I wish I had a simple answer. My short answer is our people. Our people truly and genuinely care. We believe in "moving heaven and earth" to make our guests happy but also realize that two ingredients are necessary for that to occur: culture (philosophy) and a plan. The service culture must start at the top and, through shared vision and values, permeate the entire organization. Exceptional service comes from our people and your people. At the same time it must be backed by a strong service culture, training, technology, and systems that empower us to serve. It centers on our Credo, our 20 Basics, and again, our people.

Exceptional Customer Service speaks to frontline associates, managers/ leaders, CEOs, and owners alike. It's not hype; it's real issues with real solutions . . . not to mention some great humor mixed in. It's a text that brings you the practical do's and don'ts that have made Lisa Ford's videos the best-selling training series in the United States. Whether you are a tire dealer in South Carolina, a dry cleaner in California, or a major manufacturer in the Northeast, this book can and will help you. It talks retail, it talks professional service firms, it talks business-to-business, and most everything in between. *Exceptional Customer Service* has tips, team and individual exercises, humorous cartoons, and most of all, real-life anecdotes from the authors to bring home the experiences of poor and exceptional service.

I join these authors in encouraging you to make a difference in how we serve. Begin your journey to Exceptional Customer Service today and set the standards for others to follow. You'll be glad you did!

Horst H. Schulze
President, Chief Operating Officer
Ritz-Carlton Hotels

Authors' note: As founding president and COO of The Ritz-Carlton Hotel Company, Horst Schulze revolutionized the hotel industry, creating one of the most recognizable international brands, forever altering the very nature of customer service by creating a culture of "ladies and gentlemen serving ladies and gentlemen." Today, Mr. Schulze is chairman, president and CEO of Atlanta-based West Paces Hotel Group, where he applies his considerable talent to building a new standard in luxury hotels. Visit *www.westpaceshotels.com*.

Preface

If there is a common denominator shared by all organizations, it is the critical need for exceptional customer service. In a 2008 Forrester Research report 64 percent of respondents claim that the customer experience was a "critical strategy issue." This is why we have written this book. It's a how-to with steps, tips, and exercises. It's an individual and team guidebook that provides a roadmap for changing service attitudes and behaviors. As this second edition has been updated, we realized something very profound. The art of creating exceptional experiences for customers is TIMELESS! Certainly technological advancements have been achieved over the past decade, and as before, they continue to either enhance or inhibit the personal customer experience. Research continues to focus on what makes and breaks customer experiences and loyalty—and we have shared the current studies to help you understand the trends of today.

It is difficult to think of a business that doesn't live or die by its customer focus. Even the much-maligned Internal Revenue Service has been forced through public and congressional pressure to become more customer friendly.

Thousands of books have been written on the subject of customer care. Many are excellent; some generate enthusiasm and resolve that propel one to the office the next day to revolutionize customer service. Most of these books fall short, however, in one major respect. Providing exceptional customer service requires behavior modification on the part of executives, managers, and frontline workers alike. Modifying behavior requires persistence, perspiration, and most of all, practice.

The second edition of *Exceptional Customer Service: Exceed Customer Expectations to Build Loyalty and Boost Profits* is based on a combined close to 100 years of knowledge and practical experience of the authors. What has previously been shared on video and in seminars with millions of people around the world is now in print to be taken home or to the office with practical methods of improving customer service.

In writing this book, we have taken into consideration the current trend toward flatter and more global business structures and the use of teams. We have also included the technological impacts of today, including the evolution of e-business. *Exceptional Customer Service* is not only a must-read, it's a must-use book that should not sit on the bookshelves of corporate libraries. It should be on the desk of managers and frontline associates for ready reference during team meetings, training sessions, and in the heat of battle with challenging customers.

We hope you enjoy the book, but, moreover, we hope you use it at all levels in your organization! And remember—today is a great day to get started.

Lisa, David, and Bill

For additional biographical information, refer to the authors' websites:

www.LisaFord.com
www.TheMcNairGroup.com

Lisa Ford, *lisa@lisaford.com*
David McNair, *david@themcnairgroup.com*
Bill Perry, *billp@themcnairgroup.com*

Chapter One

A Great Day to Get Started

"It's a GREAT day at Gerald's Tires! My name is Scott, how may I help you?"

This is the enthusiastic greeting you will receive when you call Gerald's Tires in Charleston, South Carolina. We begin this book by telling you a little of Gerald's story for a couple of reasons.

First, we want you to know about them because they represent the essence of creating the customer experience. Secondly, we like Gerald's because everyone can relate to them—both as a customer and as a service professional.

They are not Walt Disney World, Nordstrom, Target, Ritz-Carlton, or FedEx—the names you so often hear associated with exceptional customer care. They are a simple tire and brake store with six locations and just over seventy employees. They deliver what many perceive to be a commodity in a competitive industry, and yet they have distinguished themselves as Service Stars. The best part about getting to know Gerald's is that you can see that what they have is not magic, nor is it perfection. What they have is an organizational culture that never loses sight of the customer. Almost never anyway—and in this world that puts them in the top .00001 percent!

Meet Bill Watts, the president, and David Ard, Gerald's vice president and general manager. Better yet, meet Scott Cook, Jane, Andy, Amy, or any of the employees and you will walk away impressed! These folks have a simple philosophy—make the customer happy! In fact, you almost don't realize the planning and systems that make their customer care program work so well.

How It All Began

When you do business with Gerald's Tires, you might expect there to be someone named Gerald. It must be the owner, right? *Wrong.* Well, maybe half right. The business began when two men, Howard Watts and John Sullivan, decided to carve out a niche in the tire industry by opening a retread-only tire store. Gerald Davis was a deliveryman working for Howard at his retread manufacturing plant. When the company opened its first retail retread store, Gerald was given the opportunity to run it. He greeted the folks, changed the tires, exchanged the cash, and was even known to dispense some personal advice now and then. The store's owners thought it might be a good idea to name the store after the man who represented the business so well every day—Gerald. And was that one proud employee! Gerald ran the store like he owned it; he treated the customers like he owned it. And guess what? Customers treated Gerald like he owned it, too. In fact, as the business grew, Gerald became part owner of four stores. Gerald's legacy for personal service lives on today at these fine stores.

Inspiration with a Plan

So how do the current owners and managers of Gerald's keep the service spirit alive? How do they retain their employees at levels far above industry standards? Why do their customers keep coming back and telling their friends and neighbors to do the same? They have a plan. It's a system that begins with employee recruitment and training. It's a system that stays healthy through continuous measurement of results; and it promotes itself with attitude, communication, and a determination to always do what's in the best interest of the customer.

How They Hire

If you want a job at Gerald's, be prepared to take a personality test. A personality test to change tires? You bet. Every employee at Gerald's is screened for his or her social interaction skills. Sure, they look for organization, attention to detail, and other professional traits, but above all else, they'll sacrifice some "dotting of i's and crossing of t's" to get a person who relates well to other people. They want a person who not only enjoys people but who enjoys serving other people.

And once they find the right person they train them. The company's expectations are clear. Here are a few examples:

Phone Skills: The telephone is often the first impression made, and it's an opportunity to reinforce relationships throughout the customer experience. At Gerald's they have a script. It tells you how to answer the phone, how to use your name, how to ask for the customer's name, how many times to use the customer's name, and how many times to use the store's name. Yet with all of this, the script is flexible enough to allow an employee to inject his or her personality into the call. It is anything but robotic.

Policy Stomping: Gerald's coaches employees on certain words to use (or not use) that reflect their company's culture. For example, you better not hear an employee talk about "company policy." Customers don't want to hear about policy. Think about it. When do you usually encounter the word policy? It's most often being used defensively in some sort of service standoff.

Haven't you stood in line at the dreaded retail store return counter (often referred to as the Customer Service Desk—Ha!) and been a bit uneasy because you didn't have the receipt for your item. Possibly you were armed with your story that it was a "gift" or maybe you were prepared to lay blame on the store that they never gave you a receipt. Whatever the case, you were prepared and attentive—and the moment the word "policy" was tossed in your direction, you launched into an explanation of why it shouldn't apply to you. Rather than citing policy, isn't it better to ask the customer what they would expect in the situation or, simply put, what would make them happy or what they believe is fair?

Customer Recovery: Bill Watts, president, is the first to admit that Gerald's slips now and then. But the company doesn't take those slips lightly, and when they do occur, they are ready to make it right. Bill spends a great deal of his time coaching employees on doing what's right for the customer. "Don't call me," he says. "I'm not standing there with the customer. I'm not looking at his car, and listening to his concerns. You are. You have good judgment. Just do what you think is best."

Measuring the Customer Experience: Gerald's uses three different techniques for keeping abreast of their customers' opinions.

1. Mystery shoppers and teleshoppers—hiring "fake" customers to do business with your stores and report on their findings.
2. In-store comment cards.
3. Follow-up phone calls to make sure everything was okay.

On a day when I visited Bill at his office (a place he'd rather not be if he can spend time with folks at his stores) he grabbed a stack of comment cards from his in-basket. We flipped through them together to see what customers were saying about their experiences. I was stunned. The comment cards have a rating scale of 1 to 10, representing poor to excellent. They ask for impressions regarding prompt greeting, courtesy, wait time, etc. What I saw was 10, 10, 10, 10, 10, 10, 10! Rarely did a customer give any other rating. And when asked if they'd recommend Gerald's to a friend, not only did customers check yes, but they often wrote, "already do." Now there's a loyal following!

One gentleman wrote in on six different comment cards, "You need more benches outside." As you would expect, more benches were ordered, but so was something else. Gerald's sent the commenting gentleman a gift basket with a personal note that said, "We heard you about the benches. Come visit us and try them out. Thanks as always for your business."

And Then Some

The overall philosophy at Gerald's is give 'em what they ask for, *and then some!* In other words, don't just handle the transaction, build a relationship. Maybe it's just a more casual way of saying, "Exceed their expectations!" One thing is for sure, it works. The employees understand it, and the customers appreciate it.

One of the "and then somes" that Gerald's is most noted for is giving a rose to every female customer. It is laid on the seat of each car before pickup, and it comes with a note that expresses special appreciation for the business. Gerald's knows how intimidating car service stations can be for people, and they are constantly striving to soften the rough edges. Now think about this—a rose being given at your tire dealer! Can you picture the discussion that must have taken place as this idea was first tossed out by one of Gerald's employees? *A rose?! To every woman that brings her car in . . . are you serious?! Who's going to go* get these roses? How much will this cost? How will we keep them fresh? What if they sit in the car too long on a hot Charleston summer day—they'll look more like a flat tire than a rose! Bad idea! Fortunately, Gerald's not only embraced the idea, they also thought of ways to solve all the logistical barriers to it. And has this idea paid off? You bet. This idea has engaged their customers and created a word-of-mouth campaign that no advertising budget could replace.

The "and then somes" don't stop there. If it's not a flower, maybe they vacuum the floorboards of your car or wash your windshield and top off the fluids. The "and then somes" have led to great ideas like play areas in the waiting rooms to help entertain children, and fixing all flat tires for free! The fact is that this philosophy of service builds a creative energy that puts no boundaries on the possibilities of going above and beyond.

Pass Me the Silver Bullet

Bill is frequently requested to speak to college students, trade groups, and at various industry forums about Gerald's' service success. When he does, he's quick to point to the other 100 associates in the company who make it what it is. And finally he says, "There is no silver bullet for service. People keep looking for it. Is it the roses, the enthusiasm, the personality-based recruiting, or the countless other 'and then somes'? Maybe yes, maybe no, maybe partly. But it is the culmination of many little things—all of which are delivered with a smile."

Nothing More Than Survival

This book is about customer service. It's also about competitiveness, profitability, and, in fact, business survival. The two are really the same, and owners like Bill Watts know it. There are plenty of very good tire stores in Charleston, South Carolina. Plenty of places to go if service at Gerald's takes a nosedive.

Consider the reasons why customers go elsewhere. A number of surveys have been done on the subject including this one reported by the American Society for Quality and the Quality and Productivity Center. Here's what it showed:

Why Companies Lose Customers

Customer dies 1%
Customer moves away 3%
Customer influenced by friends 5%
Customer lured away by competition. 9%
Customer dissatisfied with product 14%
Customer turned away by an attitude
of indifference on part of service provider **68%**

That's right! Sixty-eight percent of the time that your business loses a customer it's because of poor service. If that statistic alone isn't a wakeup call, consider this one. The average company loses half of its customers every five years and doesn't even know it lost them, much less the reasons why.

As If That Wasn't Enough

Here are a few more statistics to consider:

- It costs between five and six times more to attract a new customer than to keep an existing one.
- According to research done by Bain & Company, companies can boost profits anywhere from 25 to 125 percent by retaining merely 5 percent more existing customers.

- A 2 percent increase in customer retention has the same effect on profits as cutting costs by 10 percent.
- Happy customers tell four to five others of their positive experience. Dissatisfied customers tell nine to twelve others—and who knows how many on the Internet—how bad it was.
- A study by Daniel Yankelovich revealed that two-thirds of customers do not feel valued by those serving them.

From looking at these numbers, two messages are crystal clear:

1. Exceptional customer service results in greater customer retention, which in turn results in higher profitability.
2. Most organizations haven't gotten that message yet or are ignoring it if they have.

A Bain & Company survey of more than 362 companies concluded that 80 percent believed they delivered "superior experience" while their customers only rated 8 percent of them as delivering that "superior experience." That sums up the disconnect between service delivery and the service experience! Furthermore, when Adobe Systems, Inc., teamed with the Economist Intelligence Unit (EIU) on a global survey, they discovered that eight in ten executives believe their companies lose sales each year due to failure to create customer engagement. Some believe this lack of engagement accounts for between 50 to 75 percent of lost sales! EIU's senior editor, Rama Ramaswami, said: "Executives are increasingly finding that the winning differentiator is no longer product or price, but the level of customer engagement relative to the competition."

Just Wait Until Next Week

A case in point: A *New York Times* reader named Dorothy Klein sent a story into the Metropolitan Diary section of the paper. In the story,

Ms. Klein described the scene at a large post office in Brooklyn where a long line of customers was not so patiently waiting for service. Only one window was open and the wait seemed endless. All at once, five postal workers appeared carrying a ladder, balloons, and a banner that read "Customer Appreciation Week." Slowly the workers proceeded to hang the banner. Meanwhile, the line of customers barely moved. Finally, a very frustrated man near the end of the line pointed out to the supervisor that while five workers were hanging a customer appreciation banner, people had been waiting for more than half an hour for service because only one window was open. He asked the manager, "Do you not see an inconsistency here?" "Oh that," she replied, glancing at the banner and at her work crew, "that doesn't start until next week."

Haven't we all experienced this type of situation somewhere, sometime? Or we walk into a store and immediately see a sign that reads something like, "Through these doors pass the most important people on earth—our customers!" Thirty minutes later, after searching desperately, you finally find a sales associate. Apparently, many businesses think that by simply declaring dedication to the customer that behavior will magically follow. It takes more than words and even more than the right attitude toward customers. Exceptional customer care takes a plan, a method of translating attitude into action. Bill Watts has a plan at Gerald's—it includes recruitment, training, feedback, measurement, and many other service aspects.

It's All in the Attitude

The human resource firm HrEasy Inc. surveyed 1,000 applicants for customer service associate jobs. The results were very revealing.

- 41 percent disagreed with the statement that the customer is always right.
- 25 percent said it is hard to keep a positive attitude when dealing with customers.

- 20 percent felt most customers were too demanding.
- 15 percent said that dealing with customers gets in the way of getting their job done.

Yes, you heard it right, 15 percent of a sample of 1,000 people applying to serve the public feel that the customer gets in the way. Imagine that! If I just didn't have those long lines of people and cars, imagine how many hamburgers I could make!

Business to Business

Many of the stories and examples we use in the book are retail businesses—restaurants, hotels, airlines, department stores, etc. Most of us can relate personally to the good and bad examples of their service. We've witnessed it. The principles of exceptional customer service apply equally in business-to-business situations. Supply chain management, as it is often called, involves the numerous and complex relationships necessary to fuel today's economy. Whether it's an automobile or airplane manufacturer relying on thousands of parts suppliers, a busy legal or accounting firm dependent on office machines and computer maintenance, or a hospital in need of fresh linens, quality food, and smooth working relationships with doctors' offices and health maintenance organizations, customer care is vital. In each of these examples, one or more customer-supplier relationships exists, and the nature of competition is such that business customers will "walk" just as quickly if service is poor as you and I do if we are treated rudely at a restaurant.

Lincoln Contractors Supply in Milwaukee, Wisconsin, a supplier of contractors' tools and equipment, understands this. They also understand the need for a plan. Fifteen years ago, the company implemented a "Customer for Life" business philosophy. They look at every customer and ask, "How much could this person or company spend with us over the course of their lifetime?" Lincoln doesn't want to deal with a customer just once; they want a customer's business forever.

The company has more than just a vision. It has a plan to accomplish that vision, which involves creating an atmosphere where the customer says "Wow." Here are a few things Lincoln does:

- Maintain large, clean showrooms with 20,000 items on display.
- Think of the store as a home and customers as guests. That means cookies in the showroom in the morning, pretzels in the afternoon, coffee and tea, and twenty-five-cent sodas in the soft drink machine (many contractors come in for their quarter soda and end up buying something). On hot summer days, a five-gallon cooler full of Gatorade is also available at the counter.
- Encourage the sales staff to always try to exceed customer expectations. When dealing with a challenging customer, they are told to ask the customer what is fair, then take it one step or a few dollars further—in the customer's favor.

Lincoln Contractors Supply has only one rule for the entire workforce:

**Empower your people to make decisive and
immediate customer service decisions.**

How It All Comes Together

Fast food restaurants are not generally considered bastions of great customer service in America. Of course, there are exceptions. Most are individual restaurants that stand above their average corporate counterparts. If you have ever been to a Chick-fil-A, however, you know things are different as soon as you walk in (note: the chain is not yet national). A friendly greeting, an accurately delivered order, and a sincere thank you are the minimum you get.

There are many reasons for this consistently delivered service. It starts with founder Truett Cathy, who established the company on a strong set of values. Careful hiring and orientation, rigidly enforced service standards, and generous employee benefit programs all contribute to a service culture second to none in the fast food industry.

Gerald's Tires and Chick-fil-A share many things in common in their approach to serving customers. Foremost is a passionate commitment from the top down to providing the highest levels of service every day. The chapters that follow are loaded with tools, exercises, and stories that can help transform your organization into a customer-centric one. Enjoy!

It's a Wrap

Did you catch all of the following points?

The Gerald's Tire store

- ★ A "plan" for maintaining service levels
- ★ The "people connection"
  - Hire people who want to serve others
  - Train, train, train
- ★ Emphasize the basics
  - Telephone skills—the first line of communication
  - It's our policy—NOT!
  - Customer recovery—do what's right!
- ★ And then Somes! What can they be in your organization?
  - Measure customer happiness

Customer satisfaction "by the numbers"

- ★ Sixty-eight percent of customers go elsewhere due to attitude
- ★ Customers—it costs more to get 'em than keep 'em
- ★ Unhappy customers tell nine to twelve others—and who knows how many on the Internet?
- ★ Fifteen percent of applicants for service positions say customers get in the way!

Don't forget business-to-business/customer-supplier relationships

Chapter Two

Aerobicize Your Program: Why Everyone Isn't Doing Customer Service

The term "customer service" is losing its punch. That is, the *term* is losing its punch, not the act or its impact. Customer service is no less important in today's marketplace than at any other time. In fact, the need for improved customer service is at an all-time high. It's just being called different things today . . . customer loyalty, customer engagement, customer-centric. Why? Because of the changing ways in which we conduct business. It's more about looking from the outside in, and making stronger and longer-lasting connections with those you serve. Why? Because consumers have increasingly more choices. Why? Because customers have lower levels of brand and product loyalty. Think

about it. How differently is your organization doing business today than it did five years ago?

- Most organizations are flatter, with fewer levels of management.
- Teams and self-led work groups are becoming more prevalent.
- Technology, and most notably e-commerce, is transforming communications, order, and delivery systems, radically redefining our markets.

If customer service is so important, then why aren't more businesses doing it well? One answer lies in the fact that we as customers define great (or poor) service on a personal, individual basis. That definition is based on the interaction of two variables—what we *expect* and what we *actually receive from a service provider.*

Let's say we are going to an upscale restaurant for a special occasion. We've never been to the restaurant before. Our expectations are pretty high. They are formed by a number of factors: what others say about the restaurant, reviews in the newspaper, and price being just a few.

The big night arrives and we go to dinner. The food is excellent, the service is great (but not over the top), and the atmosphere is warm and inviting. Do we define our evening as exceptional? Some may, but most of us would think, "I expected a lot and got what I expected." A great evening, but not a "wow."

Weeks later, after a long day of shopping, we stop at a small restaurant in a strip mall for a quick dinner. Again, we've never been there before, but this time we don't expect much. Well, we go in and the experience blows us away. We are seated immediately, the atmosphere is nice, the wait staff cordial, and the food some of the best we've had for the money. We leave and plot our reality much higher than our expectation. Do we consider this an exceptional experience? You bet. We'll probably even go home and tell our neighbor, "You've got to try Joe's Diner over at the mall. It's the best kept secret in town."

Two weeks later, you take your neighbor to Joe's Diner to show him personally how good it is (we all love to show off our favorite places and be seen as an expert). You receive the same service and food quality as before. Your expectation on the second visit was higher, probably about equal to your reality the first time, so you weren't nearly as impressed the second time. Your neighbor probably wasn't either, because you raised his expectations by raving about the place.

As customers, our expectations for service and product quality are constantly increasing. We are better educated and informed consumers; we have more choices and expect the best value for our money. Service we thought was great five years ago is barely satisfactory today. The better we are treated today, the more we expect tomorrow. The bar that defines exceptional service continues to be raised and, unfortunately, very few businesses have the knowledge or desire to make continuous improvements to their service programs.

The American Customer Satisfaction Index confirms this. The annual survey, administered by the National Quality Research Center at the University of Michigan, measures our satisfaction as consumers with the quality of goods and services we receive. In the baseline year of 1994, overall customer satisfaction measured just under 75. After fourteen years of measurement, the ACSI index is still just over 75. While customer expectations for service levels has risen, the level of service being *provided* has remained flat.

Consider a Typical Morning

To illustrate the poor service that we consumers are subjected to, I have chronicled a typical weekday morning. Actually it's less than two hours of a morning. You may confront many of the same type of experiences in your day.

Tuesday, 6:40 A.M. I received a bill in the mail from my previous cellular telephone provider. The bill was for one dollar. No explanation, just one dollar. I was puzzled by the bill since I had called to terminate the service more than two months prior, but I also knew it wouldn't go away by itself. My first thought was this was some quirky overage in the balance, and I should just pay it and be done. While usually opting to take the easy road, something nagged me about this and I decided to place a call to the 1-800 service number. It was a 24-hour number, which I liked. It was just before 7:00 A.M.

After a seemingly interminable wait cluttered with all sorts of recorded marketing messages and music, a customer care representative named Greg finally answered my call. Greg was able to explain the charge. This was a monthly fee to be paid for having my phone "on suspension." Oh, so that's the problem—somehow they thought my phone was suspended, not disconnected. Easy to fix? Not so fast, Ace.

Greg was happy to terminate my phone service as of today but didn't seem to grasp that I had called to terminate it sixty-three days earlier. He did show a record of my original call but held his ground that I had requested a suspension, not termination. I was just shy of feeling like Greg didn't believe me—like I was trying to sham them for a dollar. "Now let's not be silly. Let it drop. We are only talking a dollar," I thought. Of course that wasn't the point. For me, it was the principle involved. Greg said he had no way of waiving the one-dollar fee. Hard to believe, so I asked for a supervisor. None was available, but I could leave a number and be assured that someone would call me back. Enough was enough. I told Greg to terminate the service once and for all and that I would promptly send a check for the ridiculous one dollar.

At this point, some hint of past training triggered in Greg's mind. He asked me if I had already selected another cellular provider and if there was anything he could do to keep my business. "Oh no," I assured him, "the decision is final, and I think it's a good one."

As I hung up the phone, many thoughts ran through my head. Did the company so frown on terminations that the original representative purposely coded it as a suspension? Was it a simple entry mistake on the first representative's part? If it was a mistake, were there not policies for correcting it so as to please the customer? Why was I not asked on the first call how my business could be retained? Did they know this was a pricing issue? Did they think I was moving? Was it quality of service or product? One thing was for sure, the company really didn't care about my business.

7:10 A.M. the next call was to my new cellular provider. I couldn't find my mobile phone that morning when leaving the house. I usually kept it in my car, and after a thorough search of house and car, I concluded that it might have been stolen. I almost never lock my car.

Anyway, now I'm dialing another customer care center to report the loss and check on my insurance coverage. Great! A real person answered the call on the second ring. Brenda was pleasant and clear in her greeting. I congratulated myself again for having switched to this company. Uh-oh. Things suddenly started sliding downhill. First I was informed that I did not have insurance on my phone. Although I was sure I had requested it when I bought the phone, the fact was they had no record. Brenda seemed quite eager at that point to sell me a new insurance plan for my account (I couldn't help but think she had a sales quota to meet). The problem was we weren't addressing the issue that my phone was missing. I had no phone to insure. We decided it was best to suspend my service until I found my phone or purchased a new one. Again thoughts began popping in my head. How was it that I didn't have insurance from the get-go? While I could understand not being able to reinstate it retroactively, I did at least want some sympathy and recognition that this might have been their error, not mine. In the end I found my phone and added the insurance option. The company has dropped a notch on my scale.

7:40 A.M. Somewhat in disbelief, I realized that almost an hour had passed. Now I was rushed for an 8:00 A.M. appointment in town. All the traffic lights were in my favor and the day was looking up, until I pulled into the garage of the office complex where I was meeting. The garage was dark and dirty and had extremely tight aisles and spaces. I drove in circles for what seemed like ten levels before finding a space. COMPACT CAR ONLY. I guess that meant it didn't want my sport utility truck. I'd have parked in it anyway if I thought it would fit. So back down the levels I go until I finally encounter a garage attendant. "I'm running late, where can I park this thing?" I blurted as I slowed to a stop. "We're pretty full," he responded. "Don't know what to tell ya." Obviously he didn't. I wanted to hear things like "Pull over here in this reserved spot. I know she's on vacation." Or, "Leave your keys with me, and I'll find a suitable space. You can pick the keys up at the ticket booth when you return." How about, "I'm sorry this is making you late. I'll be glad to call the person you're meeting and tell them you're having trouble finding parking in our garage."

Consider that this is a "professionals" building, meaning it houses lawyers, accountants, a bank, and a brokerage firm. What impressions are being made on their behalf? How easy are you finding it to do business with them? Do you feel safe? Does the experience make you want to return?

The Answer Is Simple . . .
The Implementation Is NOT!

We ask again. If customer care is so vital to the success, not to mention the survival, of a company, why aren't more organizations doing it well? The answer is simple, but the implementation is not. Delivering exceptional customer care takes a plan, a commitment, and training, training, training! Developing an exceptional customer service program is much like developing a fitness routine. It's a workout. It's not a one-time grueling workout. It's a long-term program of constant activity. If you truly understand the positive impacts of a distinguishing service program, then you must work at it constantly and consistently.

Accountability—A Leadership Essential

Critical to understand is the role of true leadership in defining and delivering a service culture, and the importance of having organization-wide accountability for it. After all, good ideas are a dime a dozen, but it's those who can carry them through who take the lead.

While out of town recently, I walked into a grocery store to pick up a few items. It was a sizeable store and part of a national chain. Clean and organized—you bet . . . almost sterile with its bright lights and clean, reflective floors. Then I spotted him—the manager. He was fastidiously arranging bread along the shelves. And surely he too set the standard of personal appearance with his crisp blue shirt and striped tie, his pressed khaki pants, and perfectly combed hair.

But what was missing? Where was the engagement, the smile, the eye contact? Where was any shred of caring about the customer versus caring about the presentation of the store? Now don't get me wrong—presentation of the store is also critical. But I watched this guy for several minutes and never once saw him actually speak with *any* of the more than fifteen customers and seven store associates who came within his immediate vicinity. I made a point of walking within arm's length of this guy three times just to see if he might say, "Good morning" or "Are you finding everything" or how about "Welcome to our store. Just let us know if you need any assistance." He failed!

While it may be unfair to judge this whole store by the fifteen minutes I spent there, what I did notice was that not a single store associate seemed to engage—not the bakery clerk, the cashier, the stocker, or the bagger. Did I get what I came to get? Sure, but little else.

Now contrast that with my next stop that morning, which was a Caribou Coffee shop just down the street. Yes, they too are part of a large national chain of over 500 stores and 6,000 employees. The moment you entered the door, you sensed the comfort, the friendliness, and yes—the energy! They are an organization founded on passion, hard work, environmental and community stewardship—and somehow all of that seemed evident in the first ten minutes in the shop. It was almost as if the taking of orders and the transacting of cash and coffee was secondary. The staff seemed to perform this effortlessly while their energy was in their connection with every customer that entered. You could spot the regulars . . . *'Missed you Jerry, how was Houston? Glad to be home, huh? I trust you want the regular. Just grab a paper and relax, we'll bring it to you.'* Most amazing was that as an out-of-towner, I was welcomed and felt a part of the community of these Caribou caretakers. When I sat down at a table, I leaned over to the guy next to me and commented, *'What a place, you sure don't get this kind of service often.'* And he replied, *'Oh you should see it when the manager is here! I think she knows the name of every customer that's ever entered the door . . . as well as what they drink. If you like this today, try coming back tomorrow!'* Did you get that? Another customer is inviting me back! That's customer loyalty, and that's a system driven with customer accountability.

Searching for Solutions

Delivering exceptional customer care doesn't just happen. You are dealing with issues that span the entire breadth and depth of the organization. From corporate policies to phone systems to facility appearance to personal appearance, dress, tone, listening skills, energy, manners—it all can be overwhelming. Don't let it be. Follow these steps:

- Identify your primary points of customer contact.
- Examine the goals you want to accomplish for your customers.
- Determine the type of people skills and technology functions needed to accomplish those goals.
- Construct a plan that provides the tools needed to do the job well, including a well-defined training program.

Studies have reported that well over 90 percent of all customer care problems can be directly linked to managerial issues. We said "managerial" not "management" issues. The difference is that managerial relates to HOW an issue is being addressed or managed. A management issue describes WHO is addressing it. An individual employee, and certainly teams, can have a significant impact on managerial issues. To further illustrate the difference, here's a true story.

We walked into a neighborhood eatery with some friends. We were seated by a hostess we knew from previous visits. She always had a warm smile and cheerful greeting. She apologized for the short wait and put us at a table in the center of the room beneath a ceiling fan. It didn't take long before we all started to comment on the cool temperatures and the breeze of the fan. By the time our waiter approached, we were shivering. Offering help immediately, he brought a stool over so that he could reach the cord on the ceiling fan to turn it off. (Turning off the fan was a managerial issue.) We were grateful, and this helped, but only temporarily. There was a large air vent nearby that was blowing arctic air directly on our table. And it wasn't just us. We noticed others in the restaurant with cold arms crossed and sweaters pulled over. When we asked our waiter if he could adjust the thermostat, he sheepishly said he couldn't. The restaurant owner kept a lock box on the main thermostat. (This is a management issue.) Now what sense did this make? Since he was absent most evenings, what possibly could have led him to this decision? When we think of that restaurant now, we think of ice cubes and padlocks.

The Ritz-Carlton Hotel Company is a recognized worldwide leader in their industry. All employees in their organization have a $2,000 spending authority to use for the sole purpose of "moving heaven and earth" to satisfy a customer. This is called empowering the employees. This type of devotion to the customer is a culture that is lived and taught at all levels. The hotel's former president, Horst Schulze, took an active role in setting this standard of care, and it's continued with today's president, Simon Cooper. For him, they are not selling rooms and food, they are selling service!

Marriott Hotels has put together a Sweet Dreams package. It consists of a small bud vase, a flower, and some homemade cookies. Hotel staff members are encouraged to give it to customers who are having difficulties that the hotel really can't fix. For example, a guest enters the hotel complaining that she's tired, feels awful, and her four-hour plane delay didn't help. That's the cue for the staff person to send this guest a Sweet Dreams. While the hotel couldn't control the circumstances regarding this guest's day, they control how they respond to it. Better yet, when one employee noticed a guest with an awful cough, a box of cough drops was included with the Dreams package. Now that's exceptional service!

By George, I Think He's Got It

Can you stand another hotel story? This one was told to me while working with a senior executive group at a property in Virginia. This group had a financial consultant working with them, and hence he was a guest in the hotel one evening. He'd gone out that morning for an early run, came back in, and wanted to get a newspaper. Since the complimentary copies at the front desk were gone, he went by the gift shop, where there was a stack of papers by the door. Since the shop hadn't opened yet, he leaned over, picked up one of the papers, walked about twelve feet back to the front desk, and said, "I've picked up one of your papers—here's fifty cents." And the person at the front desk said, "No, I can't do that. We're two different departments, and I don't have any way to enter that into my system." Okay. He puts his fifty cents back in his pocket, puts the paper back, and walks on. He happens upon a guy cleaning out the fireplace. He's called a houseman. He's preparing the big fire in the lobby for the day. The consultant says to him, "I know the coffee shop's not open yet. Do you know where I can get a cup of coffee?" And the houseman says, "Sure, how do you take it?" "Black." "I'll be right back." The houseman goes away, comes back in a few moments with a piping hot cup of black coffee in a Styrofoam cup. "I'll be working around here for at least the next twenty minutes. When you need a refill, let me know."

Contrast the two employees. The front desk clerk was faced with something that she didn't know how to bend the rules on. If you were working that front desk, don't you think that you might have said: Now, wait a minute. Gift shop's not open, but he just gave me fifty cents. When Christine opens up the gift shop, I'll just walk over there and say, "Christine, I've got fifty cents for one of the papers."

Things You Can Do to Make a Difference!

- Think of a situation where you have felt limited by company policy or procedure in serving your customer.
- Ask your team leader what freedoms you have to go beyond this policy.
- Substitute yourself for the last customer you served. Would you have been satisfied with the service? Would you have felt the experience was exceptional in any way?
- What's one thing you will do to make a difference in the service provided to your next customer?

Training Is Sustaining

Let's begin by establishing what we mean by training. Training comes in many shapes and sizes. It is informal and formal. It's introductory and refresher. It can be fun and participative. It can be grueling and intense. It is an investment, not a cost. Most importantly, training must be ongoing!

At Lands' End, a customer care representative receives seventy-five hours of initial training before he or she is allowed to answer the first call. And the company is always looking for ways to heighten the customer experience through its training. In 2007, Lands' End piloted a new program called *Smart Service* to focus on the finer points of developing their service representatives. Great organizations realize that training is not just ongoing—it's reinventing its professional development all the time to meet both customer and employee goals. At FedEx, new employees receive five weeks of training with refresher courses every four months. Ritz-Carlton estimates that an average of $2,700 to $3,500 is spent training each employee. And guess what—their turnover is 40 percent below industry standards.

Zappos.com, the leading online shoe retailer, begins their three-week customer service training by telling the participants to forget everything they've learned. The new company associates begin with a 156-page handbook on the company's culture—and it was written entirely by the employees themselves. They quote Jimi Hendrix, and tell numerous stories from the frontline about exceeding customers' expectations. As Nick Swinmurn, Zappos Chairman and Founder, puts it, "We are a service company that just happens to be selling shoes."

More examples can be cited, but just consider this league of companies that invest in training. These companies know that it's the quality of their workforce and the appreciation of the customer that sustains their business growth. They know that employee training is one of their better investments.

Justifying the Expense

When considering training for employees, we encourage an organization to look at a quick-and-easy Return on Investment (ROI). Following is an example of what you may want to consider:

EXAMPLE: ABC Corporation ROI for Customer Experience Training

EXPENSES

- 500 employees @ 20 hours ea. of annual training = 10,000 hr @ $10/hr wage
- Include costs and travel of trainers (in this case we considered using outside professional trainers/consultants)
- Include costs of internal staff time to coordinate all training
- Include costs for all employee travel reimbursement, overtime, etc.

REVENUE GAINS/BENEFITS

- Assumes 3% reduction in turnover = 15 employees retained @ $10K saved for each as result of investing in their professional development*
- Goal: move 10% of the 40% of customers who currently rate the customer experience as good, up to an excellent. (On a company sales revenue of $5M – 10% of that is $500K in sales that we'd expect to double as a result of the heightened experience of the customers.)
- Higher productivity is another 'gain' realized through training and heightened customer experiences. Calculate your best estimate.

Society of Human Resource Managers has numerous research studies that estimate costs for turnover of organizational managers @ 1.5 to 3 times their annual loaded compensation, and .5 to 1 times the annual loaded wages for frontline staff. We assumed conservative .5 of loaded comp rate.

EXPENSES	$$
Employee training hours	100,000
Trainers/Consultants	24,000
In-house coordinator	40,000
Misc (materials, prizes, etc.)	10,000
TOTAL	174,000
REVENUES/BENEFITS	
Employee Retention Savings	150,000
Increased Sales	500,000
Higher productivity	??
TOTAL	650,000
Return on Investment	476,000

At Target, a national discount retailer, employee turnover among hourly associates was a staggering 89 percent before they began Target University. They were able to whittle that down in a little more than two years to 59 percent. This university teaches people skills, ways to deal with difficult customers, and ways to deal with some of the stressful situations that they can find themselves in. And guess what? In addition to decreasing turnover, Target also experienced increased customer satisfaction scores during the same period.

Many large companies have in-house learning centers such as Target University. We like the name "learning center" because it conveys the benefit to the employee, as opposed to "training center," which merely describes the function that is being performed.

Learning centers can have their drawbacks as well. They may tend to centralize and formalize the training function such that information is not as relevant and easy to access as it should be. Shouldn't learning be integrated into everyday activities as much as possible? This is where employee teams have a distinct advantage. You can take the initiative to include training snippets into every team meeting. Set aside ten minutes of each team meeting to discuss a service-related event or issue. This can be as simple as reviewing a very positive service event and what specifically made the difference to the customer. You could make a different person responsible each week for bringing an article of service to the meeting for discussion. Be creative, but be disciplined. Don't let this be the last item that gets squeezed off the meeting agenda. If you do, you will have said a great deal about where you place service training in your priorities. This can be a fun and productive way of involving all team members in honing their customer care skills.

Make Training Fun

Training can and should be fun, interactive, and full of challenges. At Target University they play some pretty crazy games. They have characters called Bad Mouth Betty and Hysterical Harold. At another company, they have Lowball Larry and Rude Rudy as part of their sales and service training. The challenge is to script these characters to the extreme in role-play situations so that trainees have a chance to use their skill at dealing with the outrageous. Also, consider the opportunities and positive impacts of integrating some team building into all training. One company sets up small teams within each training session. The teams periodically perform in a series of competitions, and points are earned for their accomplishments. These team exercises are sometimes totally silly, like dance, juggling, or singing competitions, and other times they are more serious "mental challenges" that review the material that has been covered thus far. Prizes for winning teams are offered.

In order to reinforce the continuous learning concept, a computer company has adopted a unique idea. Each Friday the employees put on a T-shirt that has "Well Trained" printed on the front. On the back of the shirt there is a checklist of all the training courses offered by the company. A check by the course indicates the employee's successful completion of the course. It has become a badge of honor to wear these shirts. The sales force for this company has a seven-week curriculum. It touches on everything from products to order entry. They also have courses that put them in the shoes of the customer so they can empathize with the buyers' needs and wants. As new and still inexperienced trainees, they are given a brand new box with a computer as it is shipped from the plant. They must open it, unpack it, install all programs, and have it ready to go. Tell me this doesn't build empathy for the customer. The trainees also observe customer calls to get a feel for the type of issues they will confront. They analyze these calls and learn from them.

Training does work. But remember, when you are developing customer care skills, you are most likely talking about changing individual behavior. That takes time, repetition, consistency of message, and continual reinforcement. Sounds like a fitness program doesn't it?

Following is an exercise that incorporates a number of the points covered in this chapter:

- Identifying direct and indirect customer contact opportunities
- Generating fresh ideas for service enhancement
- How to use team meetings as mini training sessions

Allow twenty minutes per exercise below.

EXERCISE: How Fit Is Your Organization?

1. Make a list of the points of customer contact within your organization. These may be face-to-face, phone, and/or written contacts such as letters, invoices, agreements, etc. Have each team member select a different point of contact where possible.
2. Each member is to monitor/observe or review one point of contact and make notes as to how that contact could have been more customer focused.

3. Bring the above observations to your next team meeting. Ask the team to share two or three examples and recommendations. Follow with open discussion as to how that contact could have been improved.

4. Vote on the best ideas and see what you can do to make the changes necessary. It may be in the form of a recommendation/suggestion to management or a team-led implementation. Do your best to determine cost and timeline for implementation.

Contact Type	What You Observed	Suggestions

It's a Wrap

Did you catch all of the following points?

Customer service is more important than ever

★ Consumers—the choice is theirs (and they have a lot!)

★ Brand and product loyalty isn't what it used to be

★ Technology and e-business are turning marketplaces upside down

★ Nobody told the service providers—76 percent customer satisfaction rating in this country

The Service Workout Program

★ It doesn't just happen—you need a plan

★ Management versus managerial issues—there's a difference

★ Put the power into empowerment

★ How can you make a difference for a customer?

Training is sustaining

★ An investment with high return

★ Do it often and make it fun

★ Don't stop or you'll get out of shape

Chapter Three

The Plot Thickens: Learning to Plot Your Path to Service Stardom

Picture this. You're strolling along on a beautiful summer evening. You've just finished a relaxing dinner, and you happen upon an ice cream shoppe. This isn't just any ice cream store. It's top of the line (hence the extra "pe" on "shop"). They have more flavors and fancy names than you could imagine. The store is bright and cheery in its design and there's a sweet smell in the air. The large array of cones is lined up before you at the counter.

Now the bubble bursts. The first person you confront behind the counter makes no effort to finish a phone conversation, one that is quite obviously personal. As she hangs up and stands before you, you feel

BULLSEYE

compelled to ask, "Are you ready to take my order?" As you begin, a young man crashes through the swinging door at the back of the shoppe—you are thinking FIRE!—then he rushes to the front door, props it open, and begins to hurl the sidewalk cafe furniture indoors in preparation for closing. You look at your watch and notice it's 7:43 P.M. "What an odd time to close," you think.

You get your waffle cone anyway and sit inside the shoppe to enjoy it. Out comes a mop and bucket of ammonia water, as employee number three begins to wash the floors while you try to enjoy your dessert. Ahh, the taste of Chocolate Ammonia Mint in a hazelnut cone! But being a good customer, you continue eating your ice cream while remembering to raise your feet as employee number three mops beneath your table. Okay, you say to yourself, you've had enough and you walk out. At least you can enjoy the ice cream in the pleasant night air. Just as you're crossing the store's threshold, you hear the counter girl shout to employees two and three, "I'm covering the ice cream now. Tell anyone that walks in that we aren't serving anymore." You check your watch. It's 7:54 P.M. You shake your head.

If Only It Weren't True

Did any of these thoughts come to mind as you read the tale of the ice cream shoppe?

- I wonder what the owner would think about this situation?
- What a shame I have no desire to go back there, even though the ice cream was delicious.
- You just can't find good help these days.
- Will these kids ever understand the meaning of work ethic?
- I wonder how long they will be in business?
- Who's in charge here anyway? Is there no manager?
- I wish I could get that ammonia taste out of my mouth.

The type of service experienced at our ice cream shoppe raises a lot of questions. Let's go through a constructive list of the issues and questions:

1. What type of hiring practices does the business use?
2. What type of training is given to employees before they begin work?
3. Have customer service expectations been made clear, and are they reinforced periodically?
4. Was a supervisor on the premises, and is a supervisor necessary?
5. Should the owner be present to monitor these activities?
6. What reward or recognition systems may have been in place to foster high levels of service?
7. Is there any method for customers to easily provide feedback on the service they received?
8. What would have been the reaction if something were said to these employees?
9. What procedures are in place to try and win back a disgruntled customer?
10. Have we quantified the extent of damage that poor service can do to future business and to profitability?

It is actually easier to do a constructive analysis with a situation we encounter rather than with situations where our customers encounter us. But don't let that deter you. This analysis needs to be done for every level of direct customer contact.

Note to team member
How does this type of analysis relate to your team and your organization? Place a check beside any questions you believe deserve attention.

Squaring Off

You can begin to define your customer service program using a traditional scattergram tool. You can do this on many levels:

- For you personally
- For your company as a whole
- For individual products or services provided by your company
- For your competitors or industry as a whole

Let's first put some definition to the squares in the graph below along with some descriptive examples that illustrate ways to use it in your own planning. Then you can begin by categorizing activities and attributes of your company, your competition, and your personal work. That's right, your personal work. You should always attempt to personalize lessons of service right to your daily work activity.

Most companies have formal business plans. A great many also have periodic strategic plans, marketing plans, and some even have specific subplans such as a communication or public relations plans. Rarely, however, do you see a customer service plan.

Consider the diagram on the next page.

Complacents (Low creativity, low implementation of ideas): Start with the lower left quadrant. This box represents the class of service providers who merely exist. They aren't rude or foreboding, yet they are not helpful or necessarily pleasant either. They are part of the "HepYa" clan, the ones who stand behind counters and yell "Next" or "Canahhepya?"

Most likely they were never trained to serve and were not hired for their love of people, yet they are not rude or abusive. A good example of this is the robot-like cashier at the grocery store. You were greeted (you think), your products were scanned and bagged, and money was exchanged accurately. You may even have heard a "thanks." But never in the process did you feel special, appreciated, or cared for. And to think that he or she may have been your only contact with a human (representing the store that is) throughout the entire grocery shopping experience.

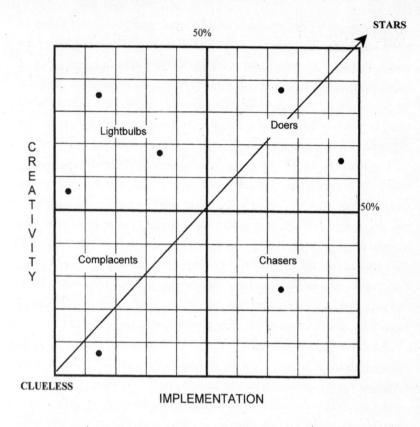

50%

C
R
E
A
T
I
V
I
T
Y

Lightbulbs

Doers

50%

Complacents

Chasers

CLUELESS

IMPLEMENTATION

Chasers (Low creativity, high implementation): Move across to the lower right box. As the name indicates, this is a more proactive group of service providers. Think again of the grocery store example. Consider when grocery stores first began express checkout lanes—the famous 12 items or less lines. This was a wonderfully fresh and welcome change that benefited the run-in shopper tremendously. It was innovative for the times. It wasn't long before all stores chased the idea. Can you think of a grocery store of any size that doesn't now offer this express service? It's no longer an innovation. If one looked for an innovation in grocery stores today, it may be their convenient parking for pregnant women or mothers with young children. It may be their electronic touch screens for locating specific products. Whatever the innovation—if it's a good one, know that the Chasers will soon pick up and copy it.

Chasers are highly attentive to what their competition or industry peers are doing. They do their best to follow suit. Their biggest problem is that they are followers, not leaders. They are implementers, not idea generators. Chasers are also not very focused, and often they can be described as "chasing their tails." For this reason they seldom leave their box of service influence. A lot of time, energy, and money can be expended by Chasers, often with little results to show for it.

Lightbulbs (High creativity, low implementation of ideas): Shift now to the upper left quadrant. This is the idea box. Creativity and imagination surge here. Ever know those people who can come up with one good, fresh idea after another? The problem is the ideas rarely go anywhere. Just think how many times you and coworkers have said, "We should just try . . ." or "If they would just develop . . ." or "I don't understand why we don't start . . ." These are "lightbulb" phrases. They indicate there is an idea out there, but it's floating. There is no true formulation, no owner, no one feeling empowered to take it and run.

If an idea flicks on a light and then it extinguishes, it's more a firefly than a lightbulb. You don't want to be in an organization full of fireflies; you want good, long-lasting lightbulbs.

An important reminder—lightbulbs should be turned off now and then. Not every idea will or should be pursued, but make sure the decision to turn off a lightbulb is a conscious one. Don't let them burn out or have others turn them off before their time.

Doers (High creativity, high implementation): Finally, move to the upper right quadrant. Now we are in the box of influence. Doers are what the name suggests. They are people and businesses of action. They not only seek ways to improve their service to customers, they act on them. They are the products of planning and training. Think of the last time you crossed paths with a Doer.

- How did you leave the transaction feeling?
- Did you comment on it to someone?
- Are you more likely to do business with them again?
- Did the experience change your impression of the company?

I recently encountered a Doer. I purchased shoes from a Bass Shoe Outlet Store while on vacation. I purchased two identical pairs, one black and one brown. I didn't take time to try on both pairs. I assumed that the boxes were marked correctly, and knowing my size, it seemed that trying on one pair was sufficient. Three weeks later I discovered I had a mixed pair—and a right shoe two sizes too large. I had thrown away the box and my receipt, and I was not looking forward to calling the store to plead for an exchange.

My expectations weren't too high. It was my fault; I hadn't checked the shoes. I'd lost my receipt and the original box. The shoes were purchased out of town weeks before. And most of all, this is an outlet store. What did I really expect? Certainly not what I got.

A young man answered the phone and introduced himself as Jason. He quickly apologized for the mistake and assured me it was the store's error, not mine. Employees are trained to check the shoes at the register to ensure correct merchandise, he said. The receipt and box were no problem. He asked if he could verify that they had my correct shoe size in stock, and could he call me back. When I requested their address to ship my mixed breed back, he was quick to set up a UPS pickup so I wouldn't be troubled for the address or the expense. Needless to say, I was impressed. Thanks, Jason and Bass, for being such Doers!

Stars: At the very point of the arrow running through our scattergram are the Service Stars. These are the organizations that consistently generate the bright new ideas and are able to see them through to implementation. They make their mark by being first with service innovations. Naturally, you can have individuals who are Stars (we devote an entire chapter to them later). You can have specific activities, products, or promotions that are Stars. The trick to being an organizational Star is *consistently* having your people, activities, products, etc. also in the Star box. Consistency is more important than frequency when it comes to being a Star.

Stars can be found in today's world, but they are not plentiful. Do not fall into the trap of thinking Star organizations are always the high-priced leaders in an industry. For example, Nordstrom is definitely considered a Star. Ritz-Carlton is another Star organization. Some might say, "They can afford to be Stars. Have you seen what they charge?" They are Stars for many reasons that have nothing to do with their rates. Most importantly, Stars can be found in any organization, in any industry, with any product or service. Here are a couple of examples.

Star Example One: The Talking Car

It was mid-August and my car's air-conditioning went on the blink. Someone recommended a dealer close to my office, which certainly was convenient. From the minute I drove onto their lot, I was impressed—clean, architecturally appealing, with very prompt and friendly service associates greeting me. I was served within minutes and then offered a ride back to the office in their shuttle. The driver couldn't have been nicer. He was a seventeen-year employee who mostly raved about how much he enjoyed his job. He was a proud employee who spoke volumes about his employer. While all of this was noticeably a step above other dealers, it wasn't Star material. But what happened next was distinguishing! When I picked up my car, I noticed a small card on the dash asking me to play the tape already inserted in my car's player. I dutifully followed instructions, and, boy, was I wowed. My service technician introduced himself and then proceeded to describe to me all that he did to my car. It was detailed, but all in lay terms that I could easily understand. He then thanked me for bringing the car to him and encouraged me to call him directly if I had any questions whatsoever about my car's service. What can I say? I've told at least fifty people about this experience. Was the work performed any better that at another dealer? Probably not. Was the price better? I couldn't tell you. Would I return there again and would I recommend it to others? You bet!

Star Example Two: The Gourmet Garage

What's to differentiate city parking garages? You enter, drive around in endless upward circles, park, pay, and leave. Wrong! Consider this special garage. Upon entering, the first thing you notice is the clean, bright colors and wide parking slots. Again, while that's nice, it's hardly Star material. But wait, as you exit your car, you notice Broadway show tunes being played—not too loud, not too soft. And here's the kicker—each floor has a different theme. The music and accompanying murals were different on each floor! A subtle yet unforgettable reminder where you parked your car. And they don't stop there. In the elevator are recorded messages telling you about the services of the garage. Need a wash, a wax, how about a quick vacuum? Just leave the keys with the attendant and your vehicle will be pampered to specifications.

In Theodore Levitt's book, *The Marketing Imagination,* he talks about the "differentiation of anything." I love that phrase. It speaks directly to the fact that nothing is a mere commodity—or at least it shouldn't be! Levitt encourages marketers to think about their products in terms of concentric rings or circles. The circles represent the state of one's product, from the innermost ring, generic or commodity-like, to a middle circle of what's expected by the customer, all the way to the outermost circle that maximizes the potential impact to the customer. This is the same concept as the *Yes . . . and then somes* that we discussed in Chapter One with Gerald's Tires. To provide the *Yes* is to give the customer what they expected from you. The Wow-factor is in the *and then somes.* It's all about being creative in how you offer your customers the surprise!

Premier Valley Bank in Fresno has redefined the traditional bank and moved to the outer circle. When you walk in the bank, you notice it does not look like a bank. Many customers even ask if they are in the right place, as there are no lines, teller windows, or a big lobby. Customers simply enter the bank and sit down at the desk of one the Business Bankers to complete their transactions. And they do not stop at that innovation—Premier Valley has a courier service that goes out to customers to pick up deposits and make change, which saves lots of employee time making trips to the bank.

Creating *And Then Some!*

Who Deserves the Credit	The "And Then Some" Event
Hospital Women's Care Center	While many hospitals have gifts for new mothers when a baby is born, this hospital in Jacksonville, Florida, sends their new families flowers one month after they've returned home from the hospital. By this time the supporting family and friends have returned to their lives. The other flowers have died, and it's a time when reality often sets in. What better time to send a gift that says we're thinking of you!
Southeastern Utility	If your electric power is not turned on the day it was promised, you'll receive a $100 check for every day it's late. While this is not printed anywhere or offered at the time the service order is placed, it's an after-the-fact commitment that builds tremendous forgiveness for the error. A utility no less? Almost unbelievable.
Bank Teller	Having noticed that many folks have dogs with them as they come through the drive-in window at the bank, this teller took it upon herself to always keep a box of dog biscuits handy.
Dentist	This dentist listened to his patients continually mention their difficulty in taking time off from work during the week for appointments. He decided to shift his hours to include evenings until eight.
Corporate Information Help Desk	When her clients have a computer problem, she's the first one they call. Not only does she work diligently to correct the problem, but she makes a follow-up call the next day to ensure all is going smoothly.
Hotel Desk Clerk	It's an everyday practice at many hotels to serve freshly baked cookies in their lobby from 5:00 to 7:00 P.M. In an Atlanta Marriott, when a tired traveler mentioned how much he appreciated them, three cookies and a note awaited him in his room the following evening.
Amazon.com	Ever place an order with them? Before you have a chance to sign off the Internet, they've sent you a response that confirms receipt of your order, the price, the ship date, and of course a thank-you for your business.
Major 800# Call Center	This center is programmed to tell you the approximate wait time for your call to be answered. Should you desire to be called back, there is even an option to select, and they will dial you back when a representative is available.

Who Deserves the Credit	The "And Then Some" Event
Going GREEN	Fairmont Chateau Lake Louise in the Canadian Rockies offers complimentary overnight parking for guests who drive hybrid vehicles.
Unbanklike Bank	Commerce Bank is open seven days a week with evening hours too. On Fridays, their deposit window is open until after midnight. What's more, it's corporate culture to always be open ten minutes before and ten minutes after stated banking hours.

Someone Has Figured It Out

There is a bank in our community that is well known for its service to customers. This bank is hardly mentioned in a conversation without someone commenting on its service attributes. In my conversation with the bank's president one day, he said, "You know, I hope all of my competitors stay around as long as my bank is around." Responding to the quizzical look on my face, he added, "They sure make me look good. If I were the only game in town, people would not recognize how special my services are." Now here is someone who has figured it out. Your customers ARE your business and they notice when you do the unexpected.

Allow fifteen minutes per exercise below.

EXERCISE: Shooting for the Stars

A. Working individually, each team member should take two minutes and list some activities or attributes of your team or organization that are Complacent. Now take another three minutes to list Doer activities or attributes for your team/organization.

Now as a group, take ten minutes to have team members describe the items on their list. See if you can discuss how some Complacent items may be changed or enhanced in order to move them into the Doer box.

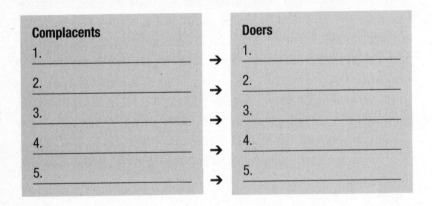

Complacents		Doers
1.	→	1.
2.	→	2.
3.	→	3.
4.	→	4.
5.	→	5.

B. Working as a team, take ten minutes to brainstorm opportunities/ideas that could move your organization into the Star box. Once you've listed the ideas, take five minutes and vote on the best ideas (we suggest no more than four or five ideas).

Service Star Ideas:

1. _____

_____

2. _____

_____

3. _____

_____

4. _____

_____

5. _____

_____

C. Finally, taking fifteen minutes, expand on realistic ways in which the Service Star ideas can be implemented. Determine specific activities that need to happen, who will be the owner of the activities, and set a date when this activity should be accomplished.

Idea	What Needs to Happen	Who	When
1.			
2.			
3.			
4.			

It's a Wrap

Did you catch all of the following points?

Plot your customer service program

- ★ You and your team
- ★ Your company
- ★ Your product or service lines
- ★ Your competitors

From Clueless to Stardom

- ★ Clueless—"The light's on but nobody's home"
- ★ Complacents—"Canahhepya?"
- ★ Chasers—"I will follow you anywhere"
- ★ Lightbulbs—"One day we should get around to . . ."
- ★ Doers—"What a great idea . . . let's start today!"
- ★ Stars—"Nobody does it better"

Look for those *Yes . . . and then some* opportunities

Chapter Four

Mirror, Mirror: A Self-Assessment

Imagine a very large mirror. Now picture yourself standing in the middle of a room looking into this wall of glass. Of course you see yourself, but we want you to look deeper. We want you to picture all of the support systems around you—all of the systems that affect the job that you do for your company or organization. And once you have a really good image, start making a list of all the support systems and people that you see in your mirror.

You should see computers, not only the hardware, but the software too. You see the lights, the phones, the policy manuals on the shelf, and you see the people that make them work. You might see accounting

BULLSEYE

and human resources folks, the sales staff, the engineers, and those responsible for making the products you sell. You may see delivery trucks and drivers, schedulers, trainers, and quality assurance inspectors. Somewhere in that reflection you see your supervisors, managers, owners, and/or shareholders. You spot the cleaning crew and facility maintenance workers. And if you look hard enough you'll see your family, friends, and significant others. Burn this image into your head and don't lose it. We ask you to do this because it's important that you realize your role in the organization and how dramatically you and the job that you do are affected by the actions and results of others.

Step through this imaginary mirror to the other side. There you will greet your customer. Whether it is by phone or face-to-face is unimportant. What is significant, however, is that this mirror, like most, is opaque on the backside. The customer cannot see all of the people behind you, she just sees you! You are the reflection of the company.

Pointing Fingers

I can still hear my mother saying, "Do not point!" as I cast my finger directly at a man who had broken the line for a ticket at the movie theater. But how else was I to make sure she knew who did this terrible wrong if I didn't point him out? As much as it angered me, that wasn't the issue for my mother. Sure, she didn't like my physically pointing, but the real issue was that I was blaming another for my situation, as if somehow that would make it better.

Now let's put that incident into the context of customer care. When was the last time a customer service representative blamed someone else for your poor service?

Event One

You have decided to buy a new leaf blower. You go to a large hardware center because you want selection and advice. You've located the lawn tools section, and, after a few minutes, you catch the attention of a salesman. This guy knows all there is to know about leaf blowers. He talks you into the battery-powered model because it's lighter to carry—easier to handle. You have a concern, however. Does it really have the power to blow leaves when they are damp or in shrubbery beds? "Of course," says the salesman. "They don't call it the little hurricane for nothing." You're sold.

It's now Saturday morning and you're trying out the "little hurricane." First disappointment and then frustration sets in. Your "little hurricane" is not much more than a hair dryer. You immediately return to the place of purchase to lodge your complaint and to upgrade your unit. And guess what you hear? "I don't know why the salespeople here keep telling people that these units have power. They don't. In fact, we must get two or three returned a week. Let me take care of this for you."

Now the customer care representative has been most helpful. Are you feeling any better about having selected this store? Unlikely. Are you feeling any better about this customer care representative? At least she's been honest. You may be feeling that it's not her fault, she's not to blame, and how unfortunate it is that she has to explain the circumstances to you. She has merely transferred any anger and frustration you may have to the salesman, the store, and even the product manufacturer. And yes, off of her. The bottom line is that you as a customer got the shaft.

EXERCISE

If you were the customer care representative, what are some things you could have said to keep the customer pleased with your store, the products, and your personal service?

Things you could have said to the customer:

1. _____

2. _____

3. _____

4. _____

Event Two

You're rushing home from work. You make a quick stop by the dry cleaners to pick up a suit for a special occasion that evening. You get home, shower, and start to dress. It's 6:30 P.M. You're okay, but with no time to spare. As you dress you notice something is not right with your suit. The collar on the front left side has what appears to be a grease smudge on it. You feel your entire mood starting to change. Why now? Why me? You change quickly but not without thinking an unkind word or two about the dry cleaners.

On the way to work the next morning you stop by the cleaners to show them the suit. The man behind the counter said, "That's the third item returned this morning with this same kind of mark on it." He goes on to explain how the suit is pressed, giving very specific information on just how the grease may have gotten there. While you may have appreciated the lesson, it hasn't done anything to solve your problem. It was yet another finger-pointing that did nothing to make you feel any better about this dry cleaners. Don't you wonder who checks the clothes before they are bagged and hung for the customers? How old is the pressing equipment? What if the stain doesn't come out? What are they going to do about it?

EXERCISE

Make a list of things that the dry cleaner could have said that you would like to have heard. Now, assume the suit doesn't come clean. List two actions that you would expect to keep you a loyal customer.

Things the dry cleaner could have said:

1. _____

2. _____

3. _____

4. _____

Actions to keep you a loyal customer:

1. _____

2. _____

While people can be at fault, it's far more critical to understand the systems behind those people. For example, did the hardware center or the dry cleaner have a plan in place to offer something to the customer for their inconvenience, cost, and aggravation? Did the dry cleaner have a maintenance schedule for the equipment? Was it someone's job to check the apparel before it went to the customer?

Over 90 percent of the problems in organizations are the fault of systems, not people. We must then ask ourselves what system could prevent this problem from occurring again. And if a system is in place, what performance review mechanism is in place for addressing it with the employee who failed to follow the procedure? The first action following a service breakdown should be a review of the system, not the fixing of blame on an associate.

Don't forget, however, that the frontline associate should be prepared with the right words to cover for a bad system. One of the best examples of this is when computers are down in a call center. Don't you get tired of hearing, "I can't check your records right now because our system is down." How about, "Let me make a note of that. Our system is updating now, but I will make that change and call you back if I have any questions at that time." Notice the difference?

How's Your Report Card

Designate some key areas of your organization and its service delivery, and have employee groups complete the report cards. It is particularly interesting to see how employees grade their own services and/or areas of the organization that affect service delivery. I find employees to be especially honest and candid in their grading. Below is a typical example of a report card that you may use. Feel free to insert your own areas of interest.

Let's Grade Ourselves . . . Just Like in School
A B C D or F (A = and then some!)

Our facilities	_____
Appearance of our people	_____
Service attitude of our people	_____
Our treatment of one another	_____

Where are your greatest opportunities for improvement?

_____

_____

Name two things that could be done *now* to improve your report card?

_____

_____

Facilities: The facilities from the parking lot to the waiting areas and/or any service areas are all important in establishing an impression for the customer. Equally if not more importantly, is the impact that the facilities have on the employee. After grading, ask WHY people assigned particular grades. For facilities, we often hear things like poor air quality in our work areas; need brighter lighting; not enough storage space; dirty and/or inoperative bathrooms; unsafe building or parking lots. It doesn't take too many report cards for the "heavy hitters" to stand out. It's important that this not be seen as a gripe session. It is an opportunity to see your organization more clearly through the eyes and ears of your employees.

When the information concerns important items like "safety" a lot can be gained from responding to the comments with improvements. It shows the employees that the company cares. Share with employees that facility modifications (be it storage space, heating & air, etc.) are not always easy to fix and can be costly. For that reason, you need to see what modifications are feasible.

Appearance: Before asking employees to grade themselves, remind them what goes into appearance—things like appropriate dress for the workplace, grooming, posture, and facial expressions. As you might guess, it's not dress but usually posture and facial expressions that get 'C' or lower grades. Use this information to talk about what can be done and how employees can be part of making a difference.

Service attitude: Employees are a little less harsh on themselves and their own organization in this area. The executives and leaders of an organization are typically pretty fair, but those frontline employees who are delivering the service tend to see themselves as 'Bs' more often than 'Cs.' When we consider that 80 percent of all service interactions are seen as *indifferent* by the customers—in my mind that's a 'C'. To get participants thinking, ask each person to write down two to three things that they do to make his or her service special, unique, exceptional. Be SPECIFIC. Look for answers like, . . . "I stand the moment a customer approaches and I walk around my desk to greet them personally and with a handshake"; "I pick five completed transactions each day and I write a personal note of appreciation to those customers"; or "I listen for what's going on in the customers day—like a crying child in the background, and I make sure to comment on how they must feel to make more of a relational or emotional connection with them." Now that's stepping up!

Our treatment of one another: This grade is typically a full letter grade lower than how they graded their service attitude. When this grade is lower, it can be a sure sign that employees don't feel supported, communicated with, or recognized for their work in the way they'd like. If participants are hesitant to speak openly about why they've given a grade of 'C' (or possibly lower), then ask them to write down suggestions for improvements and to turn them in anonymously.

Before ending this grading exercise, I like to review the overall report card given and ask employees if that's the report card they'd want to take home. It's also helpful to ask them to look at the items on the report card and comment on which one they feel is most important in delivering an exceptional experience: the facilities, personal appearance, service attitude, or treatment of one another. What you'll hear most often is the "treatment of one another" and this is correct. If exceptional support and respect for one another develops internally, it will soon translate to an exceptional service attitude.

Rewards Work, Just Ask My Dog

Once you've determined that your systems and processes are solid, it's time to look at the people part of the equation. And as we all know, one of the most important components of the "people factor" is recognition and reward.

I happen to love dogs. I also love a book by the famous dog trainer, Barbara Woodhouse, *No Bad Dogs*. "There's no such thing as a bad dog, just a bad owner." She's conveying that response follows reward. Aren't people the same? People repeat the behavior that's rewarded. It works that easily. I'm not saying we're all dogs, it's just basic nature and an instinct that we share.

Ever wonder why so many managers are stingy with praise? I find that too often we are asked to do things, we do them, and yet we don't hear thanks for a job well done. It's not that managers are bad people who don't appreciate the work. It's just that they are busy, focused on the next task, and, most likely, they were never trained in the art of appreciation. Just like outstanding customer service, this is a behavior that needs training and cultivation.

In Randstand's 2006 Employee Review, conducted by Harris Interactive, 86 percent of U.S. employees said that feeling valued is an important factor for happiness, yet only 37 percent said they feel valued in their jobs. This is unquestionably out of balance!

Praise can be easy. At Bank of Tampa, in Tampa, Florida, when a director receives a message from a fellow employee or a customer identifying a team member who provided exceptional service, a broadcast message is sent to all employees. A special gift is awarded to the employee. How simple is that—a little time and effort, that's all.

Rewards and recognition can be fun to structure. I know one group at the Department of Defense that instituted a "Mistake of the Month Award." If you catch a mistake and fix it you get a firefighter's hat as an award—a symbol that says you put out the fire. When the fire hat transfers, you get a small hat to set on your desk or computer. Some people have six or seven lined up. They love these fire hats because it shows that they went above and beyond. Naturally, recognition is powerful on both a formal and informal basis. The day-to-day 'thank you's' are always important, and we shouldn't forget the formal recognitions as well.

One year Jackson Electric Membership Cooperative in Jefferson, Georgia, held the WIT (Whatever It Takes) Awards ceremony. It was all based on the Academy Awards so seven foot tall Oscar Awards flanked the podium, Hollywood theme music played and confetti was ready along with other special effects. Employees are called up while the accolades from customers are read outlining the great service efforts. They each receive an eight-inch Oscar for the desk and a monetary award. Jackson changes the theme annually. Does this stuff work? The evidence comes with recognition from J.D. Power and Associates. Jackson EMC got the top rating due to their highest customer satisfaction score of all electric companies in the South.

If you would like some neat stuff on recognition and reward ideas, read Bob Nelson's book, *1001 Ways to Reward Employees*. You may also want to do a fresh Internet search or check your local bookstore; materials abound on this subject—certainly enough to stir some creativity of your own.

Recognition Tips

- Be specific. Thank people for something in particular such as, "I really liked the way you helped that elderly gentleman who was lost. You showed such care and compassion."
- Don't underestimate the value of small rewards. A hand-shake, note, or kind words can mean so much.
- Be timely. To point out a situation of praise at the six-month evaluation just loses its punch.
- Be sincere.
- When appropriate, make the recognition public and make it fun.

Note to team members

Recognition is not only for team leaders and other management. Think of how well it works to recognize and reward peers and other teams that you work with. Pick a team member you can recognize in the next twelve hours and use the tips above!

Another company noted for its recognition programs is Southwest Airlines. The company's former president, Herb Kelleher, is a very colorful individual. He dressed up as Elvis while helping to deal with baggage issues. He would show up regularly at team meetings. He ran numerous contests. The culture of service that Kelleher began has continued through the years. Following the tragic events of September 11, 2001, when most airlines were canceling flights and parking air-craft, Southwest maintained its loyal customer base, due largely to the personal relationships they had built with those customers through the years.

Back to Our Mirror

For the remainder of this chapter we will walk you (and/or your customer care team) through an assessment of your organization's support systems. Our focus will be specifically on those aspects that pertain to delivering exceptional customer care.

Allow fifteen minutes to complete the following tables.

EXERCISE: Mapping the Gaps I

Mapping the Gaps is a way to assess where you are versus where you believe you should be. For each area you are asked to rank the performance of your company to the statements provided. Remember, we are not pointing fingers but diagnosing system failures or gaps in your customer care program. The following rankings should be used (insert NA if not applicable):

You Must Be Joking	Maybe on a Good Day	Proud to Say That's Us
1–3	4–7	8–10

Let's start at the beginning point:

The Hiring Process

Support System for Delivering Exceptional Customer Care	Rank (1–10)	
Part of our organization's interview process directly assesses customer care skills.		
We only hire people with proven customer care experience.		
We role-play challenging customer situations with candidates.		
We provide candidates with our organization's expectations for service.		
Our orientation process includes specific emphasis on customer care.		Avg. Score
TOTAL SCORE		

TRAINING

Support System for Delivering Exceptional Customer Care	Rank (1–10)	
We have specific training that is required for all personnel involved with direct customer contact.		
We have refresher training courses on customer care at least annually.		
Each new customer care associate has an experienced mentor or buddy to whom he or she is assigned.		
Our new customer care associates monitor live customer interactions for an adequate period of time before being asked to handle them independently.		
Following the training, our performance is evaluated before we begin working with customers.		Avg. Score
TOTAL SCORE		

PERFORMANCE REVIEW, RECOGNITION, AND REWARD

Support System for Delivering Exceptional Customer Care	Rank (1–10)	
Our associates have periodic reviews made of their customer care performance.		
Feedback on performance is given in a timely and constructive way.		
Training is directly tied to the areas identified for performance improvement.		
We have an effective recognition system that highlights exceptional performance.		
Outstanding customer care delivery is rewarded in our organization.		
Our management understands the importance of exceptional customer care.		Avg. Score
TOTAL SCORE		

POLICIES & PROCEDURES

Support System for Delivering Exceptional Customer Care	Rank (1–10)	
Customers can access us 24 hours a day, 6 or 7 days a week.		
We have strong guarantees that stand behind our products and/or services.		
Our customer care associates have a reasonable "spending authority" to do what is right for the customer.		
If we disappoint a customer, we have contingency plans to help make up for the bad experience.		
Our organization conducts a Customer Satisfaction Survey at least annually.		
We track customers who have stopped doing business with us.		
We contact "lost customers" to find out why they stopped doing business with us.		
We conduct an Employee Satisfaction Survey at least once a year.		
Associates are encouraged to submit suggestions for improved service.		
Our company believes in solving the customer problem "on the spot" as opposed to referring it to another department or "up the line" of management.		Avg. Score
TOTAL SCORE		

TECHNOLOGY

Support System for Delivering Exceptional Customer Care	Rank (1-10)	
Our phone system is customer friendly.		
Our customer's first interaction with our organization is warm and inviting.		
We don't have to ask for the same customer information repeatedly when dealing with different areas of our company.		
Our information systems are up-to-date and user friendly.		
We use technology wisely to enhance, not detract from, a customer's experience.		
Customers can interact with our company via the Internet.		Avg. Score
TOTAL SCORE		

OTHER SUPPORT OPERATIONS

Support System for Delivering Exceptional Customer Care	Rank (1–10)	
Our products/services are delivered in a timely manner.		
Our advertising accurately reflects the way we do business.		
Our physical facilities are inviting to the customer inside and out.		
Signage in our facilities is pleasant and helps direct the customer.		
Our products/services are a good value to the customer.		
Our billing/invoicing is accurate and easy to read.		
We thank the customer for their business in sincere and creative ways.		Avg. Score
TOTAL SCORE		

Allow fifteen minutes to complete the following tables.

EXERCISE: Mapping the Gaps II

So how did you do? In order to evaluate yourself fairly, do the following:

1. Total your score by category.
2. If you are doing this exercise as part of a team, first calculate an average score for the team, per statement, across all tables.
3. Take the total for each section and divide by the number of statements to determine your average score per category.
4. Select your five lowest ranking statements across all categories and highlight them.

It is not easy to guide you from this assessment to implementation. Each organization is different. You may have immediate and direct control over implementing corrective action for some of the issues outlined in your exercise. You may need assistance with others, or approval before you implement changes. In the latter case, your documentation should be very helpful in making a case for system improvement.

Allow fifteen minutes to complete the following tables.

EXERCISE: Mapping the Gaps III

BUILDING A SERVICE PLAN

It would be overly ambitious to develop a fully detailed plan of action from what you have learned. You can, however, begin the process.

Select your two lowest (average score) categories from the six evaluated. Write the category in the space below and then list a minimum of three U-turn activities or ideas that would address the desired outcome.

Support System:

1. _____

2. _____

3. _____

Support System:

1. _____

2. _____

3. _____

Note to team leaders and team members

Take these exercises and ideas back to your team and or your team leader. Let them give input to the process as well. Involve at least five to seven others in the process.

Have these folks come up with their own U-turn ideas. Then, as a group, discuss these ideas. Now do three things:

1. Establish priorities for attention.
2. Assign an individual responsible for plan development and implementation.
3. Determine timetable, measurements for success, and progress report intervals.

It's a Wrap

Did you catch all of the following points?

The service mirror has two faces

- ★ Reflections—you and your support systems
- ★ The mirror image—your customer sees only you

Don't pass the blame . . . fix the problem

- ★ Customer doesn't care who, just what
- ★ Over 90 percent of problems are systems, not people
- ★ Your job: find the right words to cover for a bad system

Pavlov's people

- ★ Rewards and recognition work . . . and not just for your pet!
- ★ Tips: timely, sincere, specific, fun!

Chapter Five

Let's Talk about Me: Things You Can Do!

How do we keep ourselves going all day long? How do we keep that positive attitude? It's not easy. You have a job that, day-in and day-out never gives you a chance to regroup. You fill a lot of roles. Think about what customers expect. They expect you to be part detective, part teacher, part negotiator, part financial consultant, and often amateur therapist. It's expected that you are to be nice, pleasant, interested, concerned, empathetic—and all for eight hours a day. The fact is, this is our role. Serving customers comes with a great deal of pressure and stress.

The Wrong Side of the Bed

With all of the expectations that customers have of us, it's amazing we can even climb out of bed. We tell ourselves it's going to be a rotten day and, guess what, the day becomes that. Don't you know people who do this, people who do it almost every day? They are negative people. You walk in and say, "Good morning," and they snip back, "What's so good about it?" Learning experts tell us that 80 percent of our internal dialogue is negative.

Self-Talk

Silently talking to ourselves is normal. One of the things to help you is not less talking but less negative talking. Your self-talk can make or break how you feel about yourself, how you feel about your day, and how you feel about your customers. Positive thinking may not always work, but negative thinking almost never works!

> **Note to team members**
> You can learn much more about the effects of positive thinking in a book by Maxwell Maltz, M.D., FICS, *The New Psycho-Cybernetics.* Also check out *What to Say When You Talk to Yourself* by Shad Helmstetter, Ph.D.

Learn to listen to your self-talk. If you hear a lot of negatives, change so that it's more supportive. Think about the things we sometimes say to ourselves when beginning to deal with a customer. Be honest with yourself. We say things like: "I can't believe she goes out in public looking like that" or "Listen to that accent." Face it, we humans have biases, and these biases (sometimes prejudices) affect the way we posture ourselves in our servicing. When these negatives creep in, we fail to be as professional as we could be.

If I Were the Betting Type

There's an old concept called the 90/10 rule. Ninety percent of the things that happen to us are decent; 10 percent aren't; and we focus on the 10 percent. A good example of this is our media—especially the news media. Most tend to focus on the 10 percent that are bad to the point that we start to think the whole world is coming apart at the seams.

Now, think of your customers. The same statistic holds true for them. Ninety percent of them are good, decent folks. Ten percent go against the grain. Somehow, for some reason, we focus on that 10 percent. So I want you to start focusing on the 90 percent that are good and see if it doesn't make a difference in your life. Take the odds—go with the 90.

Tip for the Day

Don't we all know a negative person? You say, "Good morning," and they reply, "What's so good about it?" Be careful of how you let others affect your attitude, and, more importantly, try to use your own positive influence to help those around you who need it.

As I was waiting to board another overbooked flight recently, I was struck by how rude the desk attendant was to every person checking in. I further took notice when the gentleman behind me stepped up to the desk and said, "Before you help me, may I just ask why you are choosing to be so rude to everyone this morning?" The employee flicked his head back just a bit . . . paused, and then said, "I'm terribly sorry—I really have been haven't I? You deserve better." That employee earned a lot more respect from me at that moment—but what a shame that so many had received his attitude already.

The Great Escape

Let's be real. There are certain times (or with certain customers) that you need more options for keeping a smile on your face. One option that is often taken for granted is to use your breaks wisely. I am disheartened whenever I observe someone who chooses to take a break to vent (gripe is a better word) about everything that's just gone wrong in his day. Before you know it, he's almost as angry as when the incident took place originally. Don't get caught in this trap, and do what you can to get your team members out of this mode as well. It's helpful to get away from the stress of intense customer contact, but do something positive with your time. Try going for a walk, reading something enjoyable, listening to music or an inspirational tape.

Break Wisely

- Take a walk.
- Read a magazine or book.
- Listen to relaxing or uplifting music.
- Eat a snack (chocolate or fruit—it's your conscience).
- Take time for a hobby (from crosswords to cross-stitch).
- Play cards or a board game.
- Write a letter to a friend, family member, or even someone in your organization whom you admire.

Be sure you have something at your desk that evokes good feelings. These are called anchors. Anchors might include a photo, a vacation spot cut from a magazine, or fresh flowers. They help tie you to a place where you feel good.

Another way to keep the attitude up is to take care of yourself. Watch what you eat, exercise, and take up a hobby. These things have long been proven to help reduce the stress and burnout of our jobs.

And finally, bring your sense of humor with you wherever you go. One organization I know of created a humor break. The break includes a cart of fun from which party-type items are dispensed—hats, kazoos, balloons. This may sound silly, but it works wonders. It gives people a chance to relax, and it reinforces energy and positive attitude. Similarly, an environmental laboratory started a program called Save Our Sanity (SOS). It began during very busy times when employees were being asked to work unusual amounts of overtime. The company began having a cart of goodies pass through the company several afternoons a week. The cart was filled with fruits, cookies, and candy bars. It was not only a sign that the company cared and recognized the efforts being put forth, but it provided a little lift in the day for the workers.

You Versus Your Role

In your role as a customer care associate, you are the embodiment of your organization. Remember standing on the backside of the mirror in Chapter Four? All the customer sees is you. We know this, yet sometimes we let down our guard.

Recently I was sitting on an airplane. I was able to get a first class seat due to my frequent flier program and seat availability. So I'm sitting there contentedly, waiting for the flight to depart. A flight attendant breezes through the curtain from coach, approaches the cockpit, and instructs the pilot, "We need some air on back here. The sardines are starting to cook." Isn't that a revealing comment? We are paying, quite handsomely, I might add, to be on this flight, and to them we are nothing more than sardines in a box.

This type of slippage is damaging. More often than not it takes place when one employee is talking with another, and there's a customer there too. You've heard them. You're standing at a counter and one employee says to the other, "I'm going on break now," or "see you Saturday, I'm starting weekend shifts." Does this really warrant discussion in front of the customer?

Onstage and offstage

At Disney World, they don't have employees; they have cast members. And as a cast member you have a role. Whether your job is within an attraction, on stage, or behind a cash register, you clearly have a role in the Disney experience. They call it onstage and offstage.

When you are within the theme park grounds, you are there for the customer and you are onstage. And during that time you would no more break from your role than you would in delivering a script on stage. It's part of what makes the Disney experience so special.

The key to making the concept work is the offstage dimension. We've talked about the pressure and stress that come with the customer care role. It is not realistic to think that someone could stay "in role" 100 percent of the time. For these times we need a place to escape, to get out of eyeshot and earshot of the customer. Remember the importance of staying in your role. Serving customers is demanding. Keep in mind that you have many options available to help you create the customer experience. You and your customers will be happier for it.

Taking Ownership

No matter what industry you work in, or what company you work for, there will be problems. Some are caused by the company, some by the customer, some by acts of God, and some by you. It's one of those facts of life. I've always loved the message, "It's not the cards you're dealt, it's how you play them that counts." This same philosophy of living has been packaged in numerous creative ways: 100 Percent Responsibility, Own the Problem, Act Like an Owner. You've heard more, I'm sure. Like so many trite phrases, we know them but we don't live them. And why not? The improvements we would all see by living them would be astounding.

I heard a marriage counselor speak recently to a group of employees. One of the first things he would ask his couples is, "So how does your marriage work? Give it to me in percentages. Is it 75/25, 50/50?" People would come back with some split that gave him a good indication of his work ahead.

In all of his years he never once had an individual give him what he professed to be the right answer. The right answer (or the goal to strive for anyway) is 100/100. If each individual in a marriage would treat all situations as if he or she were 100 percent responsible, then most of your time would be spent thanking the other for taking care of things that you really felt you should have done. What a concept! Just imagine: "Those aren't my dishes in the sink, but I'll clean them up anyway." "The lawn is getting a little shaggy, I better mow it." "The dog needs a bath, come on, Fido!"

What if one partner starts this concept and the other continues to loaf? Don't you think after a while a little resentment would build? "Okay, I've been doing this 100 percent junk for three weeks now, and I don't see you chipping in. In fact, I think you see it as a free ride." That's not 100 percent ownership, that's keeping score. It's one of the most destructive tactics one can apply. To truly embrace 100 percent, you adopt it with no questions, no scorecard, no trial period. It's a way of life. Is this simplistic? Yes. You can come up with thousands of "yeah, but's." Can you do everything? No. Can you be taken advantage of? Yes. More importantly, however, does this philosophy provide for better outcomes and a happier existence than blaming others? Yes, yes, yes!

Now take this 100 percent ownership philosophy into your work experience and, specifically, the customer care context. Pretend you are a bank teller again. A customer just walked in and said the machine ate her ATM card. You could:

1. Tell her that she needs to fill out a new application and mail it into the customer care center three states away;
2. Tell her to go to the other side of the bank and wait for the next available personal banker;
3. Tell her she probably will save some money by not having an ATM card anyway; or
4. After showing appropriate empathy for her loss, pick up the phone, or complete the application on her behalf. You also let her know not only when to expect a new ATM card, but what options she has in the interim.

Why is the last choice selected so rarely? To the benefit of the employees—those of us trying to do right by the customer—two real things do stand in our way. First, most companies aren't structured for 100 percent ownership. By this I mean if you spent time making sure that every customer was helped to the best of your ability, you'd have a hard time getting all your work done. Furthermore, there is someone being paid by the company to do just this task, so why should you? Also, you may not have had the proper training to perform certain tasks. These boundaries have merit, but there is still ground you can pave. For example, tell the customer who *can* help them and provide the proper introduction. From a customer's perspective, think of the difference in being redirected or passed off versus being personally introduced with a recap of your needs to the person who can provide the help you need. By doing this you are taking ownership.

When I was lost in one of those major home building/lumber-to-go places and asked for help to find caulking, I was flippantly told, "Try aisle 12." Well, the "try" didn't make me feel altogether comfortable, and aisle 12 was hinges and springs for doors. Had the representative either walked with me to aisle 12, looked on a computer, or (can you imagine) offered to go get the item for me, I would not have felt like I was in this huge, impersonal warehouse.

A Few Ways You Can Take Ownership

1. How are you handling the caller who's been transferred twice already?
2. Do you actively look for people who appear lost or in need of assistance?
3. Are you detecting an uncertainty in a customer's voice that indicates he or she doesn't fully understand?
4. When you are busy, do you acknowledge the presence of a customer who is waiting and let him or her know when someone will be available?
5. Do you follow up with a customer to make sure that his or her needs were met, even if by another team member? Start your holiday gift list (it's never too early).

Taking ownership is about leaving the customer in a better condition than when the contact was first established. If the customer was frustrated, did you help calm him down and provide a solution? If she was simply transacting basic business, did you do something extra to build a relationship with her?

Don't Forget the Mission

We have discussed how demanding, repetitive, and tiring a frontline customer care position can be. But we haven't focused on the importance of MISSION. Missions are powerful when they are genuine, and when they are felt and acted upon.

I remember doing a 'mystery shop' (being an *undercover visitor*) on an Aquarium. This is one of the larger and more successful Aquariums in the county. They provide a really good experience, but over several years, they noticed that their ratings (as provided by their exiting visitors) were slipping. And they were slipping across the board—educational experience, quality of exhibits, courtesy of staff, and even their cleanliness scores were down.

It wasn't long into the mystery shop that I began to see the real issue. The facilities were truly spectacular. The exhibits were terrific and extremely clean. What was lacking was the engagement of staff. In the very first exhibit area, we found ourselves in a large room with two walls of glass overlooking a beautiful water view. I stood in the room with about forty middle schoolers waiting for their field trip to begin. The only adults joining me in the room were six teachers and parent chaperones. And then there was Becky with Visitor Services with the Aquarium. For eight and a half minutes I observed Becky to see how she performed her job. It was one of the longest eight and a half minutes I've ever spent. Becky stood along a back wall—as if she was required to hold it up. She rocked from side to side, she strolled a few feet to the left then back to the right. Not once did I see Becky interact with the children!

What is the mission of any Aquarium? Education! "To Educate . . ." appears in the mission of every Aquarium in the county. How was it that Becky missed her Mission? Why was Becky not walking the room and engaging the visitors? She could have been telling them about the special eyelids of the alligators, or the pelts of the otters, or the eyesight abilities of the hawks—the list is endless. To have done any of the above would have been living the Aquarium's mission.

Too often, organizational leaders do not take time to talk about the company's Mission. I believe it's a leader's responsibility to translate the Mission into the role of every employee.

Are You Paid Enough?

Of course not. It's a rare person in the world of frontline service who believes he is paid enough for the pressure, stress, working conditions, and challenges that go with the job. It often shocks frontline staff and managers when I wholeheartedly agree that they aren't paid enough. Frontline service can affect customer retention, customer referral, upselling, cross-selling, repeat purchases, as well as decrease returns, claims, and even stem potential litigation. Who could put a price on that?

Let me add that service and money do not go hand-in-hand. Service is delivered from the heart and it often goes to the heart. Money is a market-based transaction, and the two are not a this-for-that relationship. My point is that true service is from one person to another—whether it's an employee to coworker, an employee to vendor, or an employee to the customer—and pay should not be the motivating *or* the limiting factor. Suffice it to say—you just can't pay enough to a really exceptional service associate any more than you can put a price on a teacher who shapes a mind, a doctor who saves a life, or a firefighter who saved your most personal possessions.

Do this chart for ten to twenty contacts a day for at least two weeks.

EXERCISE: Charting L'attitudes

Use the table below or create your own and carry it with you. After each customer contact, both face-to-face and over the telephone, put a tally stroke in the row that best applies to the attitude of the customer at the beginning and end of your contact. Use the following legend as a guide for the customer's attitude:

+   customer very satisfied and happy

=   customer OK, problem resolved

−   customer was not satisfied and/or frustrated

Begin	End	Tally of Customers
+	+	
+	=	
+	−	
=	+	
=	=	
=	−	
−	+	
−	=	
−	−	

By completing this table daily, you will begin to change your behavior. At first you will notice the effort it takes to put a positive spin on every contact. Before long it will become second nature. This exercise also helps you recognize the 90 percent good versus the 10 percent not so good. At your team meetings, compare tables with one another. Talk about trends, highlights, and barriers. This chart should send you and your team members a message. What is it telling you?

It's a Wrap

Did you catch all of the following points?

The front line is the "firing line"

- ★ Stress and pressures of dealing with customers
- ★ How do you keep a positive attitude all day?

Talk to yourself—but try not to answer!

- ★ Self-talk is normal and healthy
- ★ Try and keep it positive . . . watch out for negative creep
- ★ Remember the 90/10 rule: focus on the 90 percent of customers who are great

You deserve a break today

- ★ Get "offstage" for awhile
- ★ Read, walk, snack, listen to music
- ★ Keep an attitude anchor at your desk

How are you connecting to your Mission? How do you help others connect?

Positive attitudes show (and so do negative ones)

One hundred percent ownership

- ★ "It's not my job" doesn't cut the mustard
- ★ Leave the customer in better shape than you found him or her

Chapter Six

Hello and Goodbye: First and Last Impressions

First Impressions

Business was kind of slow one very cold and rainy winter day at a luxury car dealership in Atlanta. It was just one of those dreary days when no one was anxious to venture out on the lot and show cars. Around mid-morning the silence in the showroom was shattered by the loud sputtering of an old, muddy pickup truck pulling into the dealership. The truck stopped, and out stepped a man who began walking around the lot. Probably just a "tire-kicker" out killing time, the sales team figured. After a few minutes, however, it became obvious this guy wasn't just going to look around for a couple of minutes, then leave. He was

interested in looking at new automobiles. "Who's up?" someone on the sales floor asked. "I'll pass," said one of the salesmen. "Not me," said a second. Finally, Bobby decided he would venture out and help the man in the pickup truck. You've probably figured out the story by now. The customer—we'll call him Joe—had his luxury car stolen from a convenience store parking lot a few weeks ago. All he had left to drive was his old hunting truck, and he was on a mission. After about thirty minutes, Bobby returned to the showroom with an unmistakable grin of satisfaction frozen on his face. It seems that Joe, the owner of a carpet mill, had just received his insurance settlement and proceeded to shell out $60,000 cash for a brand new automobile to replace his stolen one.

What's the moral of this true story? Be careful about forming impressions of your customers. You might be talking to Joe.

This chapter is about impressions. In the automobile story, the service providers formed a negative impression of the customer (this is a country hick who couldn't possibly be in the market for a new luxury car), and as a result no one was in a hurry to serve.

I recently shot into a popular fast food restaurant for a quick burger while on the run. While any personal service was lacking, I did not have to wait too long, and the burger did at least seem warm at first touch. (See what low expectations are set at fast food these days!) Now that I had the food, I took my tray to a side counter where drinks and condiments were available. There were three red-knobbed containers that were marked 'ketchup.' I pushed the first one—nothing happenin' there. I moved on to the second one. Nope—all out. And then to the third, and once again—nothing! Watching my frustration, a guy standing at the drink dispenser (who apparently was a regular at this eatery) said, "They never have any ketchup in those things—you have to go to the counter."

So on to the counter I went. But unless I was willing to get back in the cashier's line, I couldn't get anyone's attention. There were at least a dozen people visible to me behind that counter, but I was invisible to them. "Excuse me . . . could I . . . Um, miss . . . could you just . . ."

Finally I leaned in and almost touched the arm of a worker passing by and I said, "Do you by chance have some ketchup? It seems to be all out at the dispensers." You'd have thought I'd asked her to clip my toenails. The expression was one of disgust. And with no words at all, she reached beneath the counter and literally threw a couple of packs of ketchup (way too few for my taste) on the counter, and she was on her way to the back—never a look up, a smile, or a comment. Gone. And gone was I. I left vowing never to pay money to that establishment again, and to-date that promise has been kept. And in the line of work I do—I've had the opportunity to share that story with thousands. All because of one individual in an interaction that took less than ten seconds.

Your customers form impressions quickly about you and your business. Research reveals that we form dozens of impressions about a business and its employees within the first few minutes of our service experience. Former Scandinavian Airlines President Jan Carlzon coined the classic phrase "moments of truth" to describe these first impressions. According to Carlzon, a moment of truth occurs any time a customer comes in contact with your organization and has a chance to form an impression. It might be a greeting (or lack of one), a website, a merchandise display, a dirty restroom, how someone is dressed, or how a CSR answers the phone. Your challenge is to make moments of truth positive rather than negative.

Many of you have visited Walt Disney World in Orlando, Florida. The Disney organization does a lot of things extremely well in the area of customer service and is benchmarked regularly by organizations worldwide seeking to improve service levels. The Disney folks did some research a few years ago to determine the profile of their "average" visitor. The research showed that their visitors who traveled by automobile drove, on average, about eight hours from home to the park. The typical visiting family size was four. Now picture a hot day in the middle of the summer. Mom, Dad, and two kids are locked in the minivan for eight hours together with the refrain "Are we almost there?" echoing constantly throughout the vehicle. Disney discovered that often after the family got to the parking lot Dads (or Moms), in their haste to get the kids out and running, were locking the keys inside their cars. Being the customer-oriented organization it is, Disney World doesn't want visitors unhappy even before they walk through the gates. So they hired a crew of professional locksmiths whose sole job is to drive through the parking lots (there are a lot of them!) looking for visitors in distress and unlocking their cars—free of charge! What a positive moment of truth! Instead of inner rage at such a careless act, and thus a negative feeling at the start of their visit (or end of the day if they don't immediately realize what they've done), those Disney World visitors now have a positive image of the organization! And as a benefit to Disney, the visitors will tell dozens of friends about their positive experience.

Think of other experiences through which you have formed first and lasting impressions. Have you ever gone into a restaurant and been seated, only to notice cracker crumbs on the floor, stains on the tablecloth, or unclean eating utensils? What perception do you now have of the cleanliness of the kitchen? A negative one no doubt. You start expecting bad food, bad service, and you'll probably find it (or at least what you think is bad).

First Impressions May Start Sooner Than You Think

One day, while doing a seminar for the staff of a large hospital located in the center of a metropolitan area, I posed the following scenario: "An elderly patient has an appointment at your hospital in one of the clinics. The patient lives out of the area and will be driven in by his daughter, and this will be their first visit to your hospital. Where are those first opportunities to make a positive or negative impression on this patient and his daughter?" The first answer was "When the patient approaches the receptionist at the clinic." While the employee gave a correct answer, the *real* impression points I was looking for happened much earlier. First, the patient called for an appointment. How was he treated on the phone? Then his daughter drove him to the hospital. How easy was it to find the hospital (directional signage)? How easy was it to park? How difficult was it to find the clinic? There's four impression points before the patient has said a word to the receptionist. The lesson? First impressions start forming earlier than you think.

Make a simple flow chart of your customer process, including all the steps that a customer goes through in doing business with you. Highlight the impression points along the way. Be sure to include your web page, e-mail protocols, telephone techniques, personal contacts, and facility appearance.

Read the following example of moments of truth developed for a local motor vehicles office. Next, work individually or with your team for a few minutes and list as many moments of truth as you can think of for your own organization. Remember, a moment of truth is any opportunity for a customer to form a positive or negative impression of your organization. Be honest, and in this exercise don't concentrate so much on how you rate in each area but rather the moment of truth itself.

Moments of Truth

Department of Motor Vehicles, Anywhere, USA

1. Toll-free information number

2. Availability of forms (and pencils) in the office

3. Length of lines (see note 1)

4. Queuing method used

5. Signage in the office

6. Attitude and knowledge of DMV staff

7. User friendliness (for example, is a large sign posted listing the paperwork requirements or do you find out what documents you are missing only after standing in line for an hour?)

8. Availability of parking

9. Accommodation for the elderly or handicapped

10. Hours of operation

11. Adequacy of staffing, especially during peak periods

Note: You might think that the DMV has no control over length of lines. In South Carolina, a DMV employee team suggested several measures, since adopted, to reduce lines. Among them were two-year registrations and registration by mail (you mail in your property tax to the county and they forward the receipt to the DMV, which then mails your tags to you). The goal: to keep people from having to visit the DMV field office.

Moments of Truth

Your Organization

1. _____

2. _____

3. _____

4. _____

5. _____

6. _____

7. _____

8. _____

9. _____

10. _____

Great Expectations

In Chapter 2, we made the point that customers define service based largely on what they *received* as compared with what they *expected*. We expect certain things with regard to product and service quality. We form these expectations based on a number of factors. It may be helpful to think of them as the CARE factors:

C ompetition
A dvertising
R eputation
E xperience

Competition—If one car dealership in the area offers weekend repair service, if one airline cuts its fares, or if a maker of personal computers or digital cameras drops its prices, we expect that others will follow suit (and usually they do!).

Advertising—In television, magazines and newspapers, and the Internet, hundreds of millions of dollars are spent each year to promote products and services, building our expectations for a healthier, more comfortable lifestyle, finding the ultimate bargain, and on and on.

Reputation—Word of mouth is probably the strongest basis on which customers form expectations. "Do you know a good restaurant in the area?" "Who's the best Internet service provider?" "Who do you use to cut your hair?" These and other questions are asked and answered around the world millions of times each day. Not only do we give our recommendations on where to go (and not go) for goods and services, we use descriptions based on our most recent experience, which go a long way toward establishing the expectations of the listener.

Experience—This applies to your product, service, or organization. If you've dealt with a business in the past, you've no doubt come to expect some level (high or low) of product quality and customer service.

When the service we receive doesn't measure up to these expectations, we are disappointed. Earlier we talked about the local Department of Motor Vehicles office. They are easy to pick on because everyone has a horror story. In fairness, a great number of dedicated employees work at motor vehicles offices throughout the United States. As the late statistician and international quality guru W. Edwards Deming preached, 98 percent of problems in the workplace, be they customer service or other, are caused not by poor employees but rather by systems and procedures that are flawed. But the customer doesn't care whose fault it is. If he receives (or perceives) bad service, he'll go somewhere else if he has a choice.

When you visit your local DMV to renew your driver's license or register your car, what are your expectations for service? Mine are a long wait in line and the strong probability of having to come back a second time with more documentation. In short, my expectations are fairly low.

The good news is that it doesn't take much to exceed my expectations. Even after standing in line for forty-five minutes, if I receive courteous, helpful, and efficient service, I will leave with a more or less positive perception.

Think of some other service situations in which an expectation was created and the actual experience came up short, causing a disappointment gap. Situations such as:

- A department store has been advertising a sale (when aren't they!) with a deep discount on an item you really want. Your expectations are high. You go to the store and they are either sold out or are out of the model you want, your size, etc.
- A parts supplier that your company has been dealing with for years and that enjoys an excellent reputation delivers a crucial

shipment two days late causing you to miss a production deadline and delay a shipment to an important customer.

Map the Gap

Think of both a personal and a business example for each CARE factor where you have a high expectation set, only to find that the actual customer experience fell short, resulting in a disappointment gap.

Competition
Advertising
Reputation
Experience

Service Is Defined by Customers

What do customers want in the way of service? It's important for you as service providers to understand how customers define quality customer care, because it is against these criteria that perceptions are formed and judgments made. A survey of several thousand customers conducted by the Service Quality Institute at Texas A&M University and reported by Leonard J. Berry in his book, *Delivering Quality Service*, revealed the following six dimensions to quality customer care:

1. Reliability
2. Responsiveness
3. A Feeling of Being Valued
4. Empathy
5. Competency
6. Dealing with One Person

1. **Reliability**—Think for a minute of the businesses you frequent on a regular basis. What factor, more than any other, makes you loyal to that business? Chances are, it's reliability.

Consistency and follow through are the tickets of admission to today's competitive arena. Being reliable alone won't get you more customers, but without it you will lose customers faster than you can count. Put another way, can your customers trust you?

I travel a lot. I tend to stay in Embassy Suites Hotels or Hampton Inns because they are *very consistent* in appearance, amenities, and service. I dine at Outback Steak House, even driving a distance sometimes to find one, because of their consistent quality of service, food, and atmosphere. I always have many choices but figure "why gamble on an unknown?" I trust Embassy Suites and Outback. Most customers are like me, I think. We tend to be loyal to businesses that are consistent.

Repair service for office equipment is another good example. Most retail businesses and professional and government offices depend on quick-copy and fax machines to produce and send the reams of paper that, in spite of technology, is still the commodity that fuels every transaction. Who has not endured the frustration of hurrying to the copy machine only to find a crude, handwritten note, "OUT OF ORDER" taped on the top?

Reliability in this case means getting a repair technician on site quickly, or at least within the time frame established in the maintenance contract.

2. **Responsiveness**—Let's assume your business has passed the reliability test—your product and service is consistent, and you follow through on your promises. The next test of your ability to survive in the long term is responsiveness to the needs and wants of your customers. This means being tuned into the needs of your customers and taking action to meet and even exceed those needs—being able to *anticipate* what a customer wants or needs before they ask. I recently went into my bank over the noon hour to conduct several transactions that couldn't be performed at an ATM. One customer was being served, and I was the only person in line when I arrived. Five tellers were on duty,

while I waited five minutes to be summoned to the one teller who was accepting customers (the others were counting their money or talking among themselves). I pointed this out to my teller, who replied in a frustrated tone, "I know . . . it's ridiculous." I agree! And it is not responsiveness.

Remember the long lines for the popular rides at Disney World? Not long ago, Disney created the *Fast Pass* so you can reserve a particular time to go on an attraction. They anticipated that visitors were tired of spending much of their visit in lines and would like to maximize the value of a ticket.

Disney also has known for some time that many visitors forget where they park in the huge lots, even though it is announced on the tram. To be responsive to this customer inconvenience, Disney gridded the lot into sections (Daffy 4, Minnie 6, etc.) and began tracking the times in the morning when cars were being parked in each section. Now, all a visitor has to do is give their arrival time stamped on the parking ticket (or from memory if the ticket is in the car), and they are put on a tram to the correct section of the lot. One happy visitor was heard to exclaim, "I lost my car and Mickey found it!" That's being responsive.

3. **Feeling Valued**—Just as customers are looking for the best value for their money, they also want to feel they are valued by service providers. Here are a few examples:

- When you call a particular office supply business in Houston, Texas, and are put on hold, you are told to ask the customer care representative for a free gift because of the inconvenience.
- A furniture store in the Southeast rolls out a red carpet from their delivery truck into your living room as soon as they arrive at your house.
- The veterinarian calls your house the evening after she's treated your pet, just to make sure Angus is doing okay; or the orthodontist calls a couple days after he has put new braces on your son, just to check that they aren't too tight and causing discomfort.

Recently, two of us traveled to Richmond, Virginia, to do some service seminars. We had reservations at a hotel on the perimeter of the city. During the drive from the airport, late at night, we got lost and called the hotel for directions. Forty minutes later, upon arriving, the night clerk greeted us by name and informed us she already had checked us in and given us rooms conveniently located on the first floor. "Get a good night's sleep and stop by the desk in the morning and give us your credit card information." Wow, did we feel valued.

Mini-Exercise

Think of the last time you felt truly valued as a customer. Jot down the experience in the space below.

_____

_____

_____

How can you make your next customer feel truly valued?

_____

_____

_____

---

4. **Empathy**—Of all the ingredients to exceptional customer care, empathy is perhaps the most important, yet it is the tool most lacking in the arsenal of service associates. Not only do customers want to feel important, they want to feel that somebody cares about them and their concerns. They want to know that you are on their side, that you understand their point of view. One reason empathy is in such short supply is that it is not a skill that can be laid down in a policy or train-

ing manual or easily taught as part of customer care orientation. It is one thing to teach associates to answer a phone within three rings or say "please" and "thank you." Empathy is something that must come from inside people. Do you really care about your customers? Is it in your heart to provide exceptional service? Associates who can answer yes to these questions are committed to service and not merely following policies.

The Cold Shoulder

A woman was mugged on her way to work, and her pocketbook was stolen. Upon arriving at work one of her first calls was to a credit card company. One of the things in her stolen pocketbook was her paycheck and its invoice, with which she'd planned to pay her credit card bill. Her voice still shaking, she explained the predicament to the customer service associate who answered the phone. The customer asked if she could have a few more days to make payment without a late charge. The response of the associate went something like, "Uh huh, uh huh, uh huh, so you say you can pay next Friday." No reference to the mugging or empathy for the ordeal this customer had just been through. Just give us our money!

Contrast that situation with a customer care associate working at a call center of another large credit card company who received a very unusual request. It seems that the husband of an elderly card holder suffered from Alzheimer's disease and was missing. She had no idea where he had gone but knew that he had a credit card in his wallet, which he often used. Could the company possibly help trace his whereabouts? It would have been easy for the associate to say, "Ma'am, we can't help, but I recommend you call the police." This associate, however, felt empathy for this couple and was motivated to do more. She logged on to the company's online transaction tracking system and, sure enough, the gentleman had just made a credit card purchase at a mall about two miles away. Within minutes the elderly gentleman had been retrieved, thanks to the help of a caring call center associate. That's empathy! It is being in partnership with the customer.

5. **Competency**—This fifth dimension is really about the basics. Does your product or service meet my requirements? If I'm in a hotel room, is it clean, and can I sleep without being disturbed by noise next door? Does the product I just bought work as advertised? I recently purchased a new lawn mower from a leading retail chain. After I used it twice, it stopped working completely and wouldn't start. I loaded it into the back of my car and returned it to the store, grumbling all the way about the incompetence of the manufacturer. When I arrived, I was greeted by a very pleasant and competent sales associate who immediately figured out the problem. He personally unloaded the mower from my trunk, fixed the machine (a belt had jumped the track), explained what had happened and how I could fix it easily if it happened again, reloaded the box in my trunk, and apologized profusely for the inconvenience. Unfortunately, we don't see a lot of competence today, so that quality enables a company or service to stand out in a customer's mind. Not only was this associate competent, he took ownership of my problem and didn't pass me around.

6. **Dealing with One Person**—How do you feel when you call a business, office, or call center to ask a question or resolve a problem and get passed from person to person in your search for help, only to have to repeat your request each time? Very frustrated? Wondering why can't people take ownership?

When customers call, they want to deal with one person. Ritz-Carlton Hotels has a firm policy that any associate who hears a customer complaint owns that complaint until it is fixed. Fixing it may involve getting help from other departments, but the responsibility for follow-through and responding to the customer remains with the associate who first learned of the complaint.

Mini-Exercise

1. Which one of the customer care dimensions listed above do you feel your organization is really good at?

_____

_____

_____

2. Which one is most in need of improvement in your organization, division, or team?

_____

_____

_____

3. If your customers were sitting across the table from you, what would they say you needed to do to make them feel that your organization or team is:

Reliable _____

_____

Responsive _____

_____

One that makes them feel valued _____

_____

Empathetic _____

_____

Competent _____

_____

One that allows them to deal with one person_____

_____

Managing First Impressions

First impressions can be managed. But often we are unaware of these negative first impressions until a customer points them out to us. At a local college where enrollment was declining, a group of faculty and staff members brainstormed a list of "coffee stains" that were causing prospective students to go elsewhere. Things like:

- Only one telephone line to the admissions office, resulting in endless busy signals when attempting to get registration information.
- Financial aid procedures that were cumbersome and not user friendly.
- Poor traffic flow and signage on the campus (it was easy to get lost).

Once identified, negative impression points can be corrected. Assemble a team of associates within your organization and brainstorm a list of impressions that you feel may be causing negative perceptions by customers. Again, be honest and open.

First Impression Management

Using a team of associates, identify as many things as possible that may be contributing to bad first impressions. They may be things such as long lines, faded signs, broken promises, poor telephone techniques, lack of cleanliness, etc. For each negative impression list one action you will take to eliminate it.

Negative Impression	One Action to Fix
1.	
2.	
3.	
4.	
5.	
6.	
7.	
8.	
9.	
10.	

It's a Wrap

Did you catch all of the following points?

Moments of truth

★ It's all about first impressions—positive and negative
★ Perception is reality
★ Look out for coffee stains

Customer expectations

★ Formed based on the CARE factors
★ Disappointment gap = expectation minus reality

What customers want

★ Reliability—remember the "grandmother rule"
★ Responsiveness—tune in to your customers' needs
★ To feel valued—not just a number
★ Empathy—an inside job
★ Competency—attending to the basics
★ Dealing with one person—don't give 'em the runaround

Chapter Seven

Service with Heart: The Personal Touch

We begin this chapter with a television commercial for a major U.S. airline. The sales manager says to his sales force, "We've been dealing with our customers by e-mail, letter, phone, and fax and we've lost track of who they really are." The final scene shows the manager handing out airline tickets to the sales force to go pay personal calls on their customers, and then flying out himself to try and regain a major customer his company has just lost.

In today's fast-paced, technology-driven world, we are losing the personal touch. How many times when making a call, particularly if the news we have to give is negative, have we actually hoped that

we would be connected with a person's voice mail instead of the real person? It sometimes seems easier to leave that type of message in an anonymous manner, or just send an e-mail, allowing no opportunity for immediate feedback.

We will talk a lot more about the use of voice mail in Chapter Eleven on technology. For now, let's get down to some really basic customer skills—communication. When you think about it, exceptional customer care really means exceptional communication skills—effective listening and clearly articulating your message. Two skills, both different, but both absolutely critical to the communication process.

Let's start with listening because it is through effective listening that you can earn the respect of your customers as well as show that you understand and care about what they have to say. Identify five people you've known who really listen well. I bet you have a hard time coming up with three. Listening, as opposed to hearing, is difficult to do and requires our full attention. Too many of us spend more time talking than listening. There are "interrupters" who cut others off in mid-sentence. There are "motormouths" who don't let others even get started. Then there are the people who look like they are listening but in fact are just waiting for the first chance to express their own views. Other people appear to be listening while they're really just thinking about something else.

In customer care, the need for effective listening is even more important than in many other lines of work. It is very difficult to provide assistance to customers until you know what they need or want. Here are five steps that will help you improve.

Five Steps to Becoming a Better Listener

- Be ready to listen
- Ask the right questions
- Take notes
- Show you are listening
- Restate

Be Ready to Listen

Being ready to listen requires total focus on the customer at hand, whether in person or on the phone. You need to block out both internal and external noise before starting. Internal noise is all the self-talk in your mind. The phone rings and you are right in the middle of a project or busy closing out a transaction with a previous customer. You say to yourself, "I'm not ready for another customer yet," or "I wish this phone would stop ringing," or "Sure is a pretty day outside. I wish I was out there." You need to clear out that internal noise and focus on what the next customer has to say.

Then there is the external noise from the environment in which you work. If you're working in a call center, for example, you have the din of other associates around you, the on-hold lights blinking, or some other indication of how many callers are waiting after this one. If you are in a store, at a counter, or other "live" setting, the external noise can be even worse. Customers standing in line, an old friend walking by whom you'd really like to have a word with, a coworker coming up to ask you a question, or the telephone ringing while you are trying to serve a customer face to face (we'll talk about that in Chapter 9)—there can be lots of distractions. So clear the internal and external noise and be ready to listen. This may mean having the computer screen cleared of the last transaction and ready in front of you, or clearing your head and focusing on the person in front of you or on the other end of the phone line. The key is to focus.

Ask the Right Questions

Time is valuable, both yours and your customers'. It is important that you do everything possible to ask the right questions and get the information needed quickly and accurately. In general, there are two types of questions—open-ended and closed-ended. Open-ended questions are phrased in such a way to bring out free-flowing responses revealing wide ranges of information. They encourage the customer to explain, describe, explore, or elaborate. You may want to use open-ended questions early in the discussion or when you are fishing for exactly what the problem is. Some good examples of open-ended questions are:

- "How may I help you?"
- "Please describe the problem you are having with the . . ."
- "Can you explain to me how . . . ?"

Closed-ended questions, on the other hand, should be used to narrow the discussion and bring out specific, detailed information. Think of them much like true-false, multiple-choice, or fill-in-the-blank questions on an exam. The majority of the questions that we ask in normal conversation are closed-ended. Examples include:

- "What is your invoice number?"
- "Can you access your voice mail?"
- "Did you try installing the upgrade?"
- "What time would be convenient for us to come by?"

Sound questioning techniques can save time and increase the quality of the information you are gathering.

Take Notes

In situations where you are dealing with many customers in a short period of time, don't trust your memory—write it down or enter it on a computer screen. This is much easier to do if you are on the phone and the customer can't see you writing, but even if you are face to face, take a few notes. It helps you listen better because you are concentrating more. Don't try to transcribe the entire conversation. Listen for key words and phrases and jot them down. Even if you don't need the notes right now, they may come in handy later as you catch up on paperwork. We also recommend you use some type of standard log, form, or database—don't write notes on yellow stickies and post them all over your desk, computer, and walls. You'll lose them!

If you are dealing with a difficult customer, especially on the telephone, let him know you are writing down his concern. Say something like, "I know this is frustrating, especially after holding this long. I am concerned about the problem, and we're going to look into it for you. I'm writing this down." This lets the customer know you are concerned about his problem. Research shows that a customer is five times more confident that you will take action on a problem or complaint if you write it down than if you are merely listening. Secondly, taking notes may keep irate customers from repeating themselves over and over again.

Show You Are Listening

One of the quickest ways to kill a good conversation is for one of the speakers to lose interest. Have you ever been at a social gathering, in the middle of a wonderful conversation with someone? Suddenly you see the other person's eyes glance over your shoulder to someone else they have just spotted in the room (and want to talk to). Maybe it happens several more times during the conversation. How do you feel? Deflated? Certainly a little less engaged in the conversation than you were before.

Eye contact is only one method of showing someone you are listening. It's part of what we call "attentive silence." Head nods, attentive body position, and eye contact are all things you can do with face-to-face customers to show interest and encourage them to give you more information. Since attentive silence techniques are pretty difficult over the telephone, you need to move to what we call "attentive words." Words like "yes, I see," "uh huh," "okay," "I understand." Simply make noise every so often so the customer knows you are still on the line and doesn't have to ask if you are still there. Also, vary your attentive words a little. Don't say, "uh huh . . . uh huh . . . uh huh . . . uh huh."

Use attentive words while you are researching information for the customer. Say things like, "that screen is just about to come up," or "I'm still looking for the information." By doing this, you keep the customer from talking and bringing up unrelated issues, which may happen if he or she is uncomfortable with the silence. Put a little variety into these attentive phrases. We observed one associate in a call center who would repeat over and over, "still checking . . . still checking . . . still checking." You want to sound personal, not programmed.

Restate

In order to be an active listener you must be involved in the conversation and make sure you understand, or heard correctly, what the customer was saying. One of the best ways to do this is by restating what you heard the customer tell you. Don't repeat it word for word. That may irritate the person and make them wonder if you were listening in the first place. Just rephrase what you heard them say in your own words.

There is another reason for restating, and it's grounded in human psychology. The average person speaks at a rate of about 250 words per minute, while the average listener can listen at a rate of 450 words per minute or more. This large gap may result in inattentiveness, and you may miss important information. Ever notice while listening to a speaker that you drift in and out or start daydreaming? Either the speaker is boring or you are hearing at twice the rate that the speaker is talking. Your mind has some free time on its hands, and we all know what they say about idle minds! Restating will help you avoid missing information that you may not have heard and allows you and the customer to at least agree on the facts of the situation. For example:

"Mr. Jones, as I understand it, you are concerned about the length of time it took our repairman to arrive at your house, and would like an adjustment to the bill as compensation."

Notice several things about this restatement. First, the speaker makes no decision or takes no position on the customer's request. That comes later. Second, the speaker restates both the content and the emotion (upset). Listening for emotion, particularly over the telephone, is equally important as getting the facts. We call it "listening around the edges." People sometimes communicate things that don't come out in the spoken word. Things like frustration, anger, excitement, and pleasure come out more in tone of language and body language.

"I Shot the Store Clerk?!"

How We Communicate

Words	7%
Tone of Voice	38%
Physical Presence	55%

As the preceding chart shows, only a very small percentage of communication has to do with the actual spoken words. Ninety-three percent of any message is communicated through tone of voice and physical presence, which are visual elements such as body language and appearance (how we say something). Only 7 percent has to do to with what you say. Listening around the edges enables you to hear some of the feeling and emotion behind the words your customers are speaking. In the classic comedy movie *My Cousin Vinny*, there is a scene where a young man who had accidentally walked out of a country store with a can of tuna in his pocket without paying is suspected of shooting the store clerk. During his interrogation by the small town sheriff, the young man is so incredulous when confronted with the accusation, he blurts out, "I shot the clerk???!!!" During the trial, when the transcript of the interrogation is read aloud, it is done so in a straight monotone, making it sound like the teen confessed to the shooting rather than expressing shock at having been charged. The same words with a different tone of voice and inflection changes the meaning of the statement dramatically. Remember, if how we say something doesn't match what we say, people will only focus on the 'how' part, and the content of your message will be lost. One other note—on the telephone, the percentages change to 93 percent tone of voice and seven percent words. Just think, for example, how many different tones you can use with the simple greeting "hello." Your voice can sound friendly, hurried, angry, frustrated, helpful, and many more. Remember—watch that tone because over the phone it creates that important first impression!

There is an old saying that there's a difference between listening and waiting for your turn to talk. Which one is your habit? As we mentioned earlier in the chapter, poor listeners tend to interrupt, talk over, or not pay close attention to the customer. This is understandable. If you've worked with customers for a while, you know pretty much what they are going to say—there are patterns, be they requests for information, complaints, suggestions, etc. You may be tempted just to listen for the first few words and then start working on a solution or giving a response. Listen to the entire message. You may gain additional insight on how to sell the customer or how to solve the problem.

The Times Are A Changin'

Many years ago, well before the Internet, voice mail, automated teller machines, large shopping malls, and managed health care, life seemed a lot simpler. We walked or drove to the store, bank, doctor and were greeted by name. Shopping, getting a haircut, or cashing a check was as much a social event as it was a business transaction. People traded stories, talked about the weather, and eventually got around to conducting their business. Today, there doesn't seem to be much time for small talk and personal touches. Corner stores, house calls, five-and-dimes, and barbershops have been replaced by mega-malls, mega-mergers, home shopping networks, and online banking. As we navigate our businesses through the ocean of changes spurred by technology, massive population growth, environmental and ecological concerns, to name just a few, we need to re-emphasize the personal touch—the one-on-one contact that is the common denominator of all customer service transactions. Following are some communication basics to keep in mind.

Choose Your Words Carefully and Avoid Jargon

Even though words themselves represent only a small percentage of a message, poorly chosen words can kill communication. One of the biggest problems we observe in this regard is the use of jargon—words and phrases that you and your coworkers understand and use every day that mean nothing to your customers. Professional people—doctors, attorneys, technical support people, engineers, and accountants—are notorious for using jargon.

So avoid jargon and acronyms. I have great respect for people who can explain highly technical products and services such as computers, consumer electronics, advanced manufacturing systems, medicine, and law in understandable terms. It's part of the personal touch that helps you build a partnership with your customer.

If you have to use jargon, make sure you define the word or phrase to your customer so that he or she can explain it to someone else later if need be. Here's a tip, regardless of your profession: When dealing with customers, particularly if explaining a policy or answering a question, pretend you are talking to yourself. Then talk to that customer as you would like to be spoken to. It's a variation on the Golden Rule.

Match the Customer's Speed and Style

This strategy may appear unusual. It is extremely useful, however, in gaining rapport and building a connection with the customer. If you are serving a customer who is speaking rapidly, when it is your turn to talk, adjust your rate of speech to more or less match his. The same applies if the customer is speaking at a moderate or even a slow pace. You probably will find that you are already doing this subconsciously. If a customer is using a very simple vocabulary, modify yours so he will be able to understand your message. If she is talking to you in academic language, haul out some fifty-cent words yourself. Obviously, you will never get as slow as certain customers or as fast as others, but try and make yourself speak more like them. Take care, however, not to mimic them, especially if you are talking with someone with a foreign accent.

Match your customer in intensity of concern and emotion. Don't get angry with them if they are shouting at you, but modulate your voice to reflect your customer's intensity level. For example, responding to a customer who is obviously upset and angry using a soft tone of voice will not be as effective as saying (with an animated expression), "I understand this is a concern. If this had happened to me, I'd be angry also. I'm glad you let us know about this so we can fix it." By matching the customer's speed and style, particularly if he is angry, you can gradually bring him down in intensity by first bringing yours back down. Try it. It works!

Matching the Emotion

If the customer is	You
Natural	Are natural
Angry	Show concern
In a panic	Show a sense of urgency
Friendly	Are cheerful
Overburdened	Show sympathy
Frustrated	Are empathetic

A Picture's Worth a Thousand . . .

Research shows that people understand things more easily when some sort of picture is drawn to go along with the words. Help your customers understand in the same manner. If someone is having trouble with the format of a company invoice, for instance, show her one and explain it line by line. If the customer is on the telephone, ask her to please have the invoice in front of her. Imagine having a friend explain over the phone how to perform a complex routine on your computer. You could write the information down, then go to your computer and attempt to carry it out. Chances are you'll need to call your friend back for clarification. A better approach is to sit down at your computer and perform the functions while your friend describes the steps. Visual props are a big help in getting your customer to understand the information you are providing.

The Name Is the Game

The dictionary defines the word *rapport* as "a sympathetic relationship; harmony." That is exactly what customers want, particularly in today's fast-paced world. They want us to establish a personal relationship with them. I have frequented the same dry cleaners for several years. The services offered are pretty standard and the prices are high (that seems to be standard also). They offer drive-through service, which is convenient. What I like about the place, though, is that when I pull up and roll down the window, the attendant always greets me by name. I have no idea how all eight attendants keep track of the thousands of customer names, but I'm impressed. I feel special when I go in there, not just a number in line.

Customers love hearing their name, and you should use it whenever possible. Stay formal—Mr., Mrs., Ms., Dr.—unless the customer asks you to please call him or her by a first name. Gateway Computer Company has an interesting twist on names. When you call their toll-free number and are finally connected to a service representative, they say, "Good morning, welcome to Gateway, my name is Julie, may I have your name?" You immediately have to make a choice between giving them your first name, last name, both names, or no name. Most customers give their first name, so an informal, personal relationship is established right from the beginning of the transaction. Great idea!

Please, Let's Get Personal

Several years ago, a major hurricane struck the North Carolina coast, and mandatory evacuations were ordered for much of Florida, coastal Georgia, and South Carolina. Over two million people clogged the interstate highway system heading north out of the storm's path. What ensued was total gridlock on the highways leading out of some coastal cities. Driving times of fifteen to twenty hours for the 200-mile drive from Charleston to upstate South Carolina were not uncommon. In short, it was a nightmare!

Spartanburg, South Carolina, was my destination that day. We had four adults, two dogs, and a cat in one car for fifteen hours, mostly stop and go. When I arrived at my destination at 5:30 A.M. the next morning and wearily went into a major motel chain to claim my *reserved and guaranteed* room, I needed a little personal touch—a little empathy. Instead I was met by a rude front desk clerk who had obviously had a bad night. Before I could even get my name out of my mouth, she began shaking her head, getting ready to say, "We have no rooms." She could not have cared less that I had been driving for fifteen hours or that I had a reservation. To her, we refugees were intruders who had ruined her normally quiet graveyard shift. I had to practically beg her to check the computer, which indeed revealed I had a reservation. While I stood at the desk checking in, I heard her tell another customer, "You people have been coming in all night, and I don't know what I'm going to do!" She became angry with another patron because he didn't have a pen to sign the credit card receipt. Finally, she told another weary traveler,

"You better knock first, because there may already be someone in the room!" Incredible, but true.

Later that day a long line of complaining customers presented themselves to the manager to vent their feelings on the hideous treatment. The point? The reputation of that hotel (and, by perception, the entire chain) was severely damaged by the total lack of a personal touch by one employee. Sure it was a horrible night, with scores of unexpected guests, many without reservations. Does that excuse rude, impersonal behavior? In this case, since the associate was alone, she couldn't get "offstage" to rest, but she certainly could have called the manager, even in the middle of the night, for help.

On a positive note, the motel did something with the feedback. Several weeks later personal letters from the general manager arrived apologizing for the "unprofessional and unfriendly" behavior of the employee and requesting the offended patrons not to judge the entire organization by the shortcomings of one.

Whether you manage or work at a hotel, retail store, hospital, computer store, or manufacturing plant, the personal touch will make the difference in customer retention, and therefore, in the success and profitability of the organization. The key to personalizing your service is developing powerful communication skills. Listening, speaking, tone of voice, body language, empathy—these are much more than words. To customer Service Stars, they are important tools of the trade.

Work Your Zone

Have you ever considered the influence that you have on other people every day? In service-related jobs, most people are influencing as many as 1,000+ people each day! Often times more than 2,000 people a day! It's all part of your *Zone of Influence*.

Here's how to calculate your Zone of Influence. Estimate the number of people with whom you come in contact each day. Think about every phone call, e-mail, voice mail, and in-person contact. Now add to that number all of those people who come within ten feet of you as you move about in your day. Most people tell me their number is between 100 and 300 depending upon their job functions. Whatever your number is at this point—multiply it by 5 (and that is being conservative). Why? Because your influence extends far beyond those with whom you have direct contact. Influence by sight extends as far as thirty to fifty feet. Influence by sound extends about ten to fifteen feet. This is to say that many people are influenced by merely seeing or hearing you throughout the day, and you weren't even aware of their presence. To add further to that number, consider word-of-mouth influence. After all, people talk. People gossip. People love to share the good, bad, and ugly of things in their own day. And when they share an interaction with you—they are spreading your zone to others you may never see or know.

Calculating Your Zone

(estimate the number on a daily basis)

Number of people (coworkers & customers) you speak to	
Number of people (coworkers & customers) you pass within 10 feet	
Number of voice mails you leave	
Number of e-mails you send	
Number of letters/memos you write	
SUBTOTAL	

Number of people likely to hear your voice (in addition to above)	
Number of people likely to have seen/noticed you (up to 50 ft away)	
TOTAL	
Multiply your TOTAL by 5	x 5
ZONE OF INFLUENCE	

So as you awake for another day of work tomorrow—just keep in mind your ZONE. Remember that you are influencing one thousand or more people every day . . . about you and your organization. Make it a zone you'd be proud of!

The 10/5 Rule

One of the more powerful behaviors you can adopt is the 10/5 rule. It's something that has existed in the hospitality industry since the beginning of time, and yet it's surprising that it is not used more fully in all types of organizations.

Whenever you pass someone (coworker or customer) within ten feet of you, it is your responsibility to give this person eye contact and a smile. If you pass within five feet of someone, then you offer a personal greeting.

Is this a cultural behavior in your organization? So often I observe organizations with people passing one another, heads angled to the floor, no eye contact or greetings. And yet, we then expect the frontline of the organization to go out and be our face to the customers. How unfair and unrealistic is that expectation? When one embraces an attitude of service, it's lived 360 degrees, and without boundaries as to whether it's internal or external.

Most of us have had the experience in a fine hotel or restaurant where these greetings are standard. Immediately you feel more welcomed, more invited, and more comfortable. When the greeting comes from a housekeeper in the hallway versus the front desk personnel, it's even more noticed because it is less expected. Now step out of the hotel and into your organization. Can you see how this type of simple behavior would make a positive difference? If so—what can you do to begin to instill it? The very first step is to lead by example.

It's EASY, or Is It ESEE!

In alignment with 10/5 and your Zone is another helpful practice called ESEE (pronounced 'easy').

E = Eye Contact

S = Smile

E = Engage

E = with Empathy

Because we have already addressed the importance of eye contact, smiling, and engaging, I want to comment on the addition of "engaging with *empathy*." For some people, empathetic behavior and language is second nature. I firmly believe that we all carry some level of natural empathy. It is true, however, that empathy levels can vary greatly from one person to another. Imagine you are standing on a sidewalk waiting to cross the street. Beside you is a young mother with an infant in one hand and a grocery bag in the other. Imagine that a can drops from her grocery bag onto the sidewalk. What do you do? I have yet to meet anyone who doesn't respond that they'd pick it up. Why? The young mother didn't ask you to pick it up. You clearly do it out of empathy. You can see that her arms are full and that she'd have no easy way to handle this—so you do it for her.

Now translate this into your workplace. Can you tell when someone is in a hurry or has a sense of urgency? Can you tell when they are lost? Can you tell when they are pleased, or confused, or upset? Sure you can—if not 100 percent of the time, certainly most of the time. The minute you can spot the presence of a thought or an emotion, you have begun to realize empathy.

We now ask you to *engage with empathy*. For example, if someone appears to be lost, you could say, "This building can be quite confusing. May I assist you in any way?" If the person is dripping wet from a rainstorm that drenched them on the way in, how about saying, "How much can I thank you for braving this weather to come see us today—I'll see if I can locate an umbrella to help you to your car if it's still pouring when you're ready to leave."

Empathetic statements are taking the thoughts or feelings of the other person and putting into words what you'd like to hear if you were in their shoes. Empathy is the language of relationships. It is the connector of one person to another. It is very powerful and very underused in the service world.

I remember monitoring some calls for an electric utility's call center. A caller began by expressing the desire to change the name and billing address on the account. She interjected that her father had just passed away that week, and she was trying to have all the utilities switched to her name and address so that they'd be handled properly. You can imagine the first words out of the mouth of the utility's representative . . . *'Do you have an account number?' 'Can I verify the billing address we have on file?'* and *'What date would you like this change to take effect—our billing cycle is on the tenth of the month.'* How incredibly transactional is that?! Efficient? Maybe . . . but what happened to any sense of personal touch? Where is the relationship being formed or reinforced? Consider how much stronger the response would have been if the representative said, *'I am very sorry to hear of your father's passing, and I want to thank you for thinking of us during such an otherwise difficult time. Let me make this as easy as possible for you. If you have an account number or just his address, I can begin to make the change for you.'*

I Didn't Catch Your Name

Are you one of the more than 90 percent of people who claim you are awful at remembering names? I believe it's not that we are all so bad at remembering names—we are notoriously poor at giving our names!

When we first meet someone new, it is customary to exchange names. Now think about this . . . we pass names in the first seconds of meeting someone, and often it is while shaking hands, and often we overlap each other's greetings. Imagine the huge number of things that your mind is taking in at this point. The brain is receiving messages visually, audibly, and sometimes through touch (such as a handshake or pat on the shoulder). The visual messaging alone can clutter the brain with recognition of the other person's gender, race or ethnicity, apparel, hair style or color, jewelry, etc, etc. Audibly, the brain is registering tone, accent, pace of speech, etc. And if shaking hands, the mind is making note of firm shake, loose shake, cold hands, large hands, etc. And again, it is at this point of mind engagement that we also toss in our name. It simply gets lost in the clutter.

We have three clear tips for improved name giving:

1. *Wait to give your name until the second or third full sentence of engagement.* Example: 'So glad to see you back with us. We have some exciting new things since you were here last. As a reminder, my name is Jean, and I'm available if you need further assistance.'

2. *When you state your name, say it at about half the speed of your normal pace of speech.* It may sounds silly at first to you, but it's greatly appreciated by the person who is trying to "catch" your name. (Slow passes are easier to catch!) If you are giving your first and last name, be especially careful not to run them together. Because our names are our own we tend to rattle them off at bullet speed and expect others to connect.

3. *Where appropriate—wear a name badge.* A badge is a great reinforcement for those that may have forgotten your name. Do not rely on your badge as the sole manner by which you provide your name. You should give your name to others and let the badge be the reminder. Name badges should be worn in the high shoulder area (preferred right shoulder) at all times. Due to our American culture of handshaking it's easiest to see a name badge on the right shoulder.

The 3 Cs

Most any service experience can be dissected into the 3 Cs: Competency, Courteousness, and Care. These are fundamentals in most any service-related interaction, and they build on each other. The foundational or first-level 'C' is competency. If you're not competent at your job, customers will seek alternatives. It is the base level that establishes the perception of the customer. In other words, if you go to a restaurant for lunch, and the counter or serving staff is very nice, but the order was all mixed up or delivered way beyond expected time frame—chances are, you're not going back. They were not competent in their core line of work. Now imagine that the competency was there, but the serving staff was rude. It is highly likely that you would not return.

However, what happens most often (about 80 percent of the time) is that the service is both competent and courteous. This level of service *satisfies* the customers, and they would tend to rate the overall restaurant a 3 or 4 on a 5-point scale. So what does it take to get a 5? It takes the third 'C' or care! Without a sense of caring, the service lacks personalization and relationship. Most service personnel see their job only being about competency and courtesy. They are unaware of the power of 'care' being expressed in their relationship with the customer. Think about how 'care' can enter into this simple lunch experience. What if the counter person or serving staff brought your sandwich and said, "I've doubled-wrapped your sandwich since you're taking it to go. This will keep it warm so it will be more enjoyable when you're ready to eat." Or, "Are you dining alone? We have a nice selection of magazines and newspapers available if you'd like to pass the time. I'll bring your drink right away." These are just a couple of the infinite possibilities as to how 'care' can be expressed to begin an exceptional experience.

Allow fifteen minutes to complete the exercise.

EXERCISE: Listening to Yourself at Work

Instructions: Over the next several weeks, take time after dealing with a customer to fill out this self-evaluation form. The customer interactions may be face to face or over the telephone. Take some time at a team meeting to discuss your evaluations with other team members and solicit their feedback.

On a scale of 1 to 10, with 10 being the highest, rate yourself on these qualities:

1. Did I project interest and friendliness?   1 2 3 4 5 6 7 8 9 10

2. Did I take the initiative in helping solve the customer's problem?   1 2 3 4 5 6 7 8 9 10

3. Did I use the customer's name at the beginning and end of the exchange?   1 2 3 4 5 6 7 8 9 10

4. Was my overall tone positive, with mostly positive word use?   1 2 3 4 5 6 7 8 9 10

5. How much of my tone was negative? Less than 33 percent negative word use?   1 2 3 4 5 6 7 8 9 10

6. How was my body language? Did I allow it to give a negative perception to the customer?   1 2 3 4 5 6 7 8 9 10

7. Did I listen a lot and let the customer do most of the talking?   1 2 3 4 5 6 7 8 9 10

8. Did I show empathy for the customer when it was called for?   1 2 3 4 5 6 7 8 9 10

9. Did I avoid using jargon or terms my customer couldn't understand?   1 2 3 4 5 6 7 8 9 10

10. Did I thank the customer for his or her business?   1 2 3 4 5 6 7 8 9 10

It's a Wrap

Did you catch all of the following points?

Listen to the voice of the customer

* ★ Listening versus hearing
* ★ Five steps to becoming a better listener
  * • Be ready to listen
  * • Ask correct questions
  * • Take notes
  * • Show you're listening
  * • Restate what you heard
* ★ Listen to tone of voice and body language

The communication basics

* ★ Watch your words and avoid jargon
* ★ Match the customer's speed and style
* ★ Match the intensity of concern and emotion
* ★ Visual aids help
* ★ Let's get personal—name-calling is good (the customer's, that is)

Chapter Eight

Telephone Skills: Connecting the Call

In Chapter 6 we talked about first impressions that turn customers off even before they get to know you. The telephone is certainly one of the biggest opportunities customers have to form perceptions, either positive or negative, about your organization. In many cases the phone is the first contact that customers have with your business. And in the age of automated telephones, it doesn't take much to be a hero—simply have a live voice answer.

A new call center on the East Coast set one of its primary service tenets in its call centers as answering each call with a live voice after the

BULLSEYE

NORTHERN HEMISPHERE MUTUAL INNNNSURANCE, ...WHERE OUR CUSTOMERS mean the WORLD TO US. HOLD, PLEASE...

He can HOLD ON. So...GO ON!... THEN WHAT HAPPENED?

McNair/Nation

first ring. Although they don't always achieve that goal, particularly during peak call periods, when they do, customers are impressed.

Most of you spend a lot of time on the telephone and probably talk with a lot of customers (and potential customers) every day. Each call is an opportunity to do one or more of the following:

- Provide information and assistance to a current customer or client, thus enhancing their loyalty to your organization. If the customer is unhappy, the call may mean the difference between retaining or losing that person.
- Gain a new customer or client for your organization. In many businesses, particularly in service industries, potential customers shop around using the phone book, newspaper ads, or recommendations from friends. These "cold calls" are opportunities to distinguish your business from the competition and perhaps gain a customer for life.
- Sell additional products or services, either improved/enhanced versions (upselling), or related ones (cross-selling). For example, a customer inquiry to a pest control service about a one-time spraying may lead to an annual maintenance contract. An inquiry to a bank about current interest rates could result in a new account or other financial services.

To emphasize the power of the telephone and the importance of good telephone skills, we urge you to maintain a log for a day or two similar to the following one. The log will enable you to keep track of the types of calls you are receiving as well as opportunities to gain new customers or sell additional products or services. You might be surprised at the positive impact you make on the business.

Customer Name: _____ ❑ Internal   ❑ External

Contact #: _____

Other Contact:_____

Notes: _____

_____

Referred to: _____

Follow-up Needed: _____

Customer Name: _____ ❑ Internal   ❑ External

Contact #: _____

Other Contact:_____

Notes: _____

_____

Referred to: _____

Follow-up Needed: _____

Customer Name: _____ ❑ Internal   ❑ External

Contact #: _____

Other Contact:_____

Notes: _____

_____

Referred to: _____

Follow-up Needed: _____

Cut or bend right corner of page after all follow ups have been closed.

Making the Connection

Think of each telephone call you receive (or make) in terms of four critical stages: greeting, gathering, responding, and renewal. The length of each stage will vary according to the type of call. However, no step should be omitted. Each serves a different purpose, and each is important to the success of the call.

Greeting

In every telephone call, the greeting sets the stage. Whether you are initiating or receiving the call, there are some basics you should observe:

1. Remember the 3 Ps. Be pleasant, professional, and positive. If you do nothing else, follow the 3 Ps. Post this phrase above your phone: "Smile. They can hear it."

2. Speak clearly. Enunciate your greeting so the listener can hear what you said. There are few things more annoying than callers running the words in their greeting together. One of the reasons this frequently happens is the greeting is too long. We try to squeeze in the time of day (good morning, afternoon, etc.), the name of the business, sometimes a tagline, ("Where service is our middle name"), our name, and a greeting such as "How may I help you?" In our haste to get through it we run the words together. This is deadly because it kills the sincerity of the greeting. Review your greeting carefully, eliminate any unnecessary phrases, and then enunciate clearly and with enthusiasm.

3. Respond to the caller by name. If you are initiating the call, you will obviously know the customer's name. If you receive a call, listen carefully for the name and respond at your first opportunity using the last name. Be careful of pronuncia-

tion, however. If the name is difficult to pronounce and you are not sure about it, clarify with the customer. She will appreciate your interest in getting her name correct.

Here are some additional tips for the greeting stage of the call:

Check your mood, energy, and attitude. Before you pick up the phone, give yourself a quick attitude check and summon your energy. Remember, on the phone a lot of the energy level you may have gets lost in the telephone lines. You have to make an extra effort to convey enthusiasm and vigor.

Note to managers and team leaders

You may want to consider recording actual customer conversations. Let employees listen to the tapes privately as feedback on such things as rushed greeting, lack of energy and enthusiasm, tone of voice, and other important elements of the phone conversation.

Assess your caller. What's her mood? Upset? Frustrated? Confused? Listen for words, tone, and inflection. Many customers are direct and to the point. They have no particular mood; all they want to do is transact their business with you, get off the phone, and get on with the next task. Be sensitive to those types of callers as well.

React with sensitivity. Tailor your greeting to the mood of the caller.

Empathize with their need to call you. Let's say you work in the claims processing section of an automobile or home insurance company. Not many people will be calling you in a great mood! Most were just in an accident, suffered damage to their home through fire, tornado, hurricane, or other natural disaster, or were just robbed. You need a little empathy.

Transferring the Caller

Part of the greeting stage is a decision on whether it is necessary to transfer the call. You answered it, but you may not be the one who can help the customer. In general, it is best not to transfer callers, especially if they've already told their story to someone else. Customers don't want to deal with another person. They want just one voice. They want you to take ownership of their problem or request. Nonetheless, it is necessary from time to time to transfer callers. Here are some do's and don'ts:

Transferring a Caller

1. State what you *can do*, not what you *can't.*
2. Avoid using the word *transfer.*
3. *Brief* your coworker before passing the call.

---

1. State what you can do for the customer, not what you can't. For example, instead of saying, "I can't help you, but I'll transfer you to Mary," say, "I can help you by letting you talk to Mary. She'll be able to help you with that." Almost the same words but a much more positive message.

2. Avoid using the word transfer. Instead say, "Let me connect you with Mary," or, "Let me put you in touch with John." The difference is subtle, but the word transfer has a finality to it that may give the customer the feeling he or she is about to be dropped into a dark hole. Remember, perception is reality.

3. Brief your coworker before transferring the caller. Summarize the conversation and let the customer know you've done so. Have you ever been transferred one or more times trying to get some information only to have to start over with each succeeding person in explaining the reason for your call? It's frustrating, and it eats up valuable time.

A good transfer would go something like this:

Associate 1: "Mrs. Jones, why don't I let you speak with Mr. Johnson. I'm going to brief him on your question before he picks up so he will be better able to assist you. May I please put you on hold?" (Obviously you can only do this if you know Mr. Johnson is available. Under no circumstances should you ever "dump" a caller into someone else's voice mail during the transfer process.)

Associate 2: "Good afternoon, Mrs. Jones, this is Mr. Johnson. Thank you very much for holding. I understand you have a question about our sales returns policy. How may I help you?"

Again, it would be better if associate number one can answer the question, but that's not always possible. Should you have to transfer a caller, at all costs avoid doing it more than once. If you cannot help the customer after two tries, take his or her number and call back with an answer. You should also review your policies and procedures to determine why it took so much effort to answer the question. It would also be wise to make a written note of such difficult-to-answer questions and use the feedback later to determine if a trend exists.

Gathering

Once you have properly greeted the customer and set a positive tone for the phone call, it's time to get to work answering the question or solving the problem. Before you can do either, you must gather as much information as possible from the customer. Refer to the last chapter on listening skills, because that's what you are doing in this stage of the call. Here's a review of the basics:

- Be ready to listen.
- Be ready to take notes.
- Show you are listening through attentive silence and attentive words.
- Ask questions.
- Restate what the caller said in your own words.

Responding

After listening carefully to the customer's question, problem, or angry statement and understanding what issue needs to be addressed, it is time for you to respond. In general, you have three options:

1. Answer the customer's question or solve the problem immediately. This is the best option. Time and experience with your organization, ongoing training in products and services, and clearly articulated and publicized policies and procedures are all factors that will increase the percentage of calls you are able to resolve immediately. We all know the sense of frustration and helplessness we feel when new in a job and every telephone inquiry is an adventure. Telephone call centers realize this and most don't put new associates on live calls for some period after they start. At National Car Rental's reservation centers, for example, new associates work in an area known as "the bridge," where the ratio of associates to supervisors is four to one. These new associates field live calls; however, help is just seconds away.

2. Place the customer on hold and seek a quick answer from a team leader, or someone in the know. Like it or not, you won't be able to answer every customer question based on your knowledge, experience, or the notes in front of you. Remember that someone around you does have the answer. To get answers for your callers, you must first buy some time by placing them on hold. Before requesting assistance, be sure the information the customers need isn't right in front of you. In most cases today, you will have a number of automated databases available at your fingertips. Use them! If you can't find the information, ask a coworker or team leader.

3. Will You Hold, Please? Here are a few tips for placing a caller on hold.

- **Ask for permission.** "Will you please hold?" Or even better, if you have been talking with the customer for awhile, "Mr. Brown, would you mind holding for a moment while I get an answer to your question? I'm expecting it to be two or three minutes—will this be okay for you?" Be specific with expected time frames and check if this is okay. Nothing disappoints more quickly than being asked to hold for a moment—and that moment turns into an eternity in the mind of the customer.

- **Wait for the response.** Don't push that hold button until the customer agrees to your request. There is another reason for this besides common courtesy. The customer may not have time to wait and would rather you research the problem and call her back. At least give her the option.

- **Watch the clock.** Don't ever leave someone on hold for more than forty-five seconds unless you stipulated an agreed-upon time. If you don't have an answer in that time, come back on the line and provide an update. If customers have something to listen to like soft music (no promotional ads, please) and get an update regularly, they will stay on hold a little more patiently.

- **"Thank you for holding."** Say this each time you come back on the line. Don't say, "I'm sorry you had to hold." In the first place, you're not really sorry, and secondly, if they are unhappy with holding, you give them an opening to vent their feelings.

Renewal

The final stage of the telephone call is one that very few businesses train their associates to take full advantage of. That's a shame, because it is as important or more important than the greeting. Just as the greeting sets the tone and provides a first impression for the caller, the renewal presents an opportunity to create a lasting impression that may mean the difference in retaining the customer. Think of the renewal phase as your opportunity to invite the customer back. Here are some tips on closing out a telephone call.

Be personal, not programmed. How many times have you been talking on the telephone with a company representative and the call ends with something like, "Thank you for calling XYZ Company, haveaniceday" (pronounced as one word). Click. What lasting impression does that leave with you?

Stay away from closures that sound standard. Most telephone call centers, for example, develop scripts for their associates to follow, particularly in the opening and closing phases of the call. While these standard opening and closing phrases ensure consistency in the message from one associate to the next, they can sound deadly dull to the customer. Service Stars find a way to inject a bit of their own personality into the script, even if just in tone of voice or inflection. I have been on the phone with call center associates who, once they found out where I lived, made some reference to having visited my city or having relatives here, or simply saying, "I would love to visit your city sometime. I've heard it's a great place." Whether you have any intention of ever visiting isn't important. The important thing is to make a personal connection with the customer.

Ask if anything else is needed. Always end calls by asking customers if there is anything else you can help them with. This lets the customer know you are interested in him or her, not in a huge hurry to get off the line (even if you are), and want to help the customer as much as possible. Secondly, it may lead to more business for your company. When you call an 800 number to reserve a room at a major hotel chain, how do call center associates almost always end the call? "May I help you with any other reservations today?" or, "Do you need a rental car for your visit?" Obviously, they are not saying those things just to help you out. They want your business!

Repeat your name. One of the last things the customer should hear is your first name repeated for them. "Again, my name is Kim, and if there is anything else I can help you with, please call again." Chances are, if they ever call back, they won't remember your name and will be dealing with another associate. That's not the point. Remember, you are trying to connect with the customer, inject your personality into the call, and establish a positive perception in the customer's mind about doing business with your firm.

Most important, thank the customer for their business, and thank them personally. "We're so pleased you chose us for your Internet service." "I see that you have been a customer for three years and know that you have plenty of choices. Thank you for continuing to do business with us." These and other similar closings serve to renew the important relationships with your customers every time they call.

A Few Closing Thoughts

Many of you spend a large portion of every workday on the telephone with customers. Most of your phone calls are routine. Some callers are very friendly and interesting; a few are angry, upset, even rude. Regardless of the type of call or caller, for many customers the telephone is the way they form their first impression of the organization you work for and represent.

Telephone skills often become so second nature to us that we forget to pause and reflect on how we come across over the phone lines. Take the tips in this chapter to heart. Post them over your phone and think about them from time to time. They will help you be a true professional on the phone.

EXERCISE: Evaluating Your Telephone Technique

Instructions: Give this form to a coworker or team leader and ask them to fill it out while monitoring your telephone technique. After the call is complete, ask them to review the evaluation form with you.

Assoc. Name: _____ Date: _____ Evaluator: _____

Circular Call	E	A	MS	NI	U	NOTES
A. Greeting						
Proper Greeting						
Professional						
Positive						
Empathetic						
B. Gathering						
Readiness						
Listening Skill						
Key Fact Find						
C. Review/Respond						
Restate Need						
Offer Assistance						
D. Renewal						
Resolution						
Step Up						
Thank You						
Proper Close						
E. Total Score						

E = Exceptional A = Above Average MS = Meets Standard NI = Needs Improvement U = Unacceptable

Call Difficulty:	Easy	1	2	3	4	5	6	Difficult
Customer Began:	Positive	1	2	3	4	5	6	Negative
Customer Ended:	Positive	1	2	3	4	5	6	Negative
Closure in One Call:	Yes	No						

It's a Wrap

Did you catch all of the following points?

The telephone . . . what an opportunity to

- ★ Provide information and assistance
- ★ Gain new customers
- ★ Up-sell and cross-sell

Connecting the Call

Greeting—sets the stage

- ★ The three Ps: pleasant, professional, positive
- ★ Speak clearly and be concise
- ★ Use the customer's name
- ★ "Attitude check" before picking up the phone
- ★ Transfer calls with care

Gathering—Get to work

- ★ Listen, listen, listen
- ★ Information is gold
- ★ Take good notes

Responding—you have options

- ★ Answer the question/solve the problem immediately
- ★ Place customer on hold and find the answer
- ★ "Will you hold, please" tips: be specific in your time frame and check if it's OK

Renewal—create a lasting impression

- ★ Be personal
- ★ Avoid standard closures
- ★ "How else may I help you?"
- ★ Thank customers for their business

Chapter Nine

Customer Right-eousness: Dealing with the Challenging Ones

How many times have you heard the phrase "The customer is always right"? Whoever said that never had to deal with customers! A more accurate statement might be, " The customer is always the CUSTOMER." The customer always thinks he or she is right, and that is all that matters in the customer service business. If we want to keep customers coming back, we must treat that perception as reality.

Most customers are great. They are friendly, understanding, and tolerant. They are also knowledgeable, demanding, conscious of the value of their time, and hold high expectations for quality of product and service. You as service providers should never take them for granted.

They are the ones who make your jobs rich, rewarding, and, hopefully, profitable. On the other hand, even when customers are wrong, you must respect their perception.

Why do customers get angry in the first place? Put yourself in their place. You are, after all, a customer too! What makes you angry or upset? Chances are the same things that press your hot button have the same effect on your customers. By focusing a bit on these issues you can reduce your stress and headaches. Let's look at a few reasons customers become upset with a business.

- Expectations not met
- Someone was rude
- Someone was indifferent
- No one listened

1. Customer did not get what was expected. I recently contracted to have my two-story frame house spray washed to get rid of dirt and mildew. The house washer, a pleasant, professional young man with a good reputation, arrived early one morning and began the job. About twenty-four hours after the house was cleaned (it was spotless!), I noticed that most of our plants and shrubs were dying. When I called the company, the gentleman informed me that due to low water pressure in my housing area, he had doubled the bleach solution to compensate and make sure that the upper part of the house was cleaned. I had the cleanest house on the block, but the landscaping looked like nuclear winter had set in. I certainly didn't get what I expected.

Thousands of examples could be given of expectations not met. Who hasn't been in the drive-through lane of a fast food restaurant, ordered and received food, driven home, opened the bag, and discovered either wrong or missing items?

The solution? Raise the quality of your product or service or, in some cases, make sure the customer is clear in advance what to expect. Think back to my house-washing experience. I could have covered my plants with plastic had I known they were in imminent danger of extinction!

2. Someone was rude. Nothing can make a customer angry more quickly than rudeness. Many times the customer is perceiving, not receiving, rude treatment. Doesn't matter! Again, perception is reality in the customer service business. A newspaper I write for had an account for years with a photo shop next door. We bought a lot of film and had a lot of pictures developed there. One day, as I dropped off some negatives, the owner told (not asked) me to have our business manager come down and see him about a delinquent invoice. When she arrived in the store a few minutes later, he blurted out (in earshot of numerous customers), "Ah, Business Journal bookkeeper accountant lady, come into my office to discuss your account." Was she embarrassed? Was he rude? Did we cancel our account? Did the owner care? The answers are "yes, yes, yes, and NO!"

Ever been to the customer service desk of an airline just following cancellation of the last flight to Anywhere, USA? With frustration at a fever pitch, and tempers as short as summer in Alaska, the mere statement, "I'm sorry, we've had to cancel the flight because the engine fell off," might be perceived as rude behavior by some.

The solution? Read on. We'll give you some practical advice later in this chapter on how to deal with challenging customers without resorting to rude behavior.

3. Someone was indifferent. Have you ever asked a question of a service provider and been greeted with, "I don't know, I just work here," or "That's our policy." Words, actions, and attitude of front-line service people frequently communicate a "can't do, can't help you" message to customers.

The solution? Make sure your associates feel like a part of the team and give them the authority and support to make a difference with customers. While Horst Schulze was the worldwide president of Ritz-Carlton, every employee at every new hotel heard personally from him about the mission, vision, and values of the hotel, as well as his high service expectations. What's more, Ritz employees, from manager to bellhop, are empowered to make things right for customers, even if it means spending some money to do it. It's a powerful message. And it works!

4. No one listened. The following letter was actually written by a friend to the corporate headquarters of a home video company. The customer never received a reply to his feedback other than a one-line "Thanks for your letter." That's not listening.

Dear Sir,

It is 9:15 P.M. Friday night and I have just gotten home from one of your video stores. Going to this particular location is something that my family and I have done on a regular basis for the last 10 years. When we first started to patronize the store, it was a xxxxxxxxxx Video Store. We chose this store because, unlike the xxxxxxxx Video nearby, this store did not require me to fill out a credit application revealing my personal income for the privilege of renting a DVD. I had, and still have, a difficult time understanding why my personal income is something a clerk needs in order to determine if I am worthy of having ten dollars worth of credit extended to me. The reason for this letter is to give you some feedback on how your employees are treating customers.

When I tried to check a movie out tonight, the clerk asked me for my name. After I told her my last name, she asked for my first name. When I told her it was Doug, she asked if it was Louise. To this I responded, "No, that is my wife's name." The clerk then asked me if my name was Mark, to which I answered, "No, that is my son's name." She then informed me that I was not eligible to check out the movie unless she called my wife or son to see if it was all right. It did not matter that I had been checking out videos for 10 years. As you can imagine, I was a bit disappointed in the way I was treated and decided that the time in my life when I had to be given permission for those sorts of things had long passed.

Are your clerks not allowed to practice common sense? I am a 46-year-old, bald-headed, overweight certified public accountant. I have worked in the same job for the last nine years and lived in the same house for 12 years. I hardly have the appearance of someone who would pose a serious threat to one of your DVDs. My income is sufficient to support one son in college and another in private high school. I only tell you that as further indication of my ability to abstain from doing something for which you might regret if your employee were to rent me a movie.

Your mission, "To be a global leader in rentable home entertainment by providing outstanding customer service . . ." was hardly furthered by your employees tonight. If you do not believe customer service and common sense are paramount in a service industry like yours, you most assuredly will be in for a long ride. If you are interested in doing something about this all too important shortfall, I will be happy to share with you the name of a person whom, I truly believe, can provide you with valuable insight into how improvements can be made in this area.

Yours truly,

The solution? Listen carefully and with empathy, then do something with the feedback.

Okay, you've done everything possible to be pleasant, to listen, and to meet your customers expectations, and they are still upset. Now what? Satisfying even the most challenging customers is a critical skill. Most of us are pretty good at dealing with customers when they are rational, reasonable, and logical because we can analyze situations, provide facts, and give information and technical answers. The problem is that challenging customers don't respond to logic with logic; they respond with emotion. In fact, the more logical we become, the angrier they get. The only solution to this dilemma is to deal with emotions (theirs and yours) first. The brain won't process logic until the anger and frustration are put aside. Here is a proven five-step strategy for dealing with challenging customers.

Dealing with Challenging Customers

1. Stay calm yourself.
2. Let the customer vent.
3. Deal with emotion first.
4. Avoid emotional trigger words.
5. Delay action or consult a second opinion.

---

1. **Present yourself in a calm manner.** If you can't remain calm in the heat of battle (and often it is very difficult to do), forget the first four steps and go right to number 5, where you hopefully can bring a second person who is calm into the situation. If you believe you are capable of presenting a calm manner, here are two techniques for staying calm:

Remember the acronym STOP.

S—**Signal**. How do you feel when you first start to grow angry? Does your jaw clench or heart pound? Do you feel suddenly warm or experience sweaty palms? These and other feelings are your early warning signs that anger is setting in. Be aware of them.

T—**Take control** by . . .

O—Doing the **Opposite** of your early warning signal. Drink some water, dry your hands, unclench your jaw, or take a deep breath. Deep breathing, for example, keeps your voice opened and relaxed, nor rushed and panicky.

P—Finally, **Practice**. Being aware of your early warning signals and how best to deal with them won't guarantee that you stay calm but will sure increase your odds. If you don't know your early warning signals, ask a coworker or family member. They probably do!

Self-talk

Listen to your self-talk. Remember earlier in the book when we discussed the power of self-talk? When you find yourself dealing with challenging customers, you will really be utilizing those self-talk skills. When confronting an angry or upset customer, it is very likely that you are saying (to yourself) such things as: "Who do they think they are?" "I don't have to stand here and take this," or "I can't believe anyone would keep going on like this." This type of self-talk only serves to make you angry. Try changing that internal voice into phrases such as

"This customer must really be having a bad day to be acting like this," or "I hope I don't sound like that when I'm upset." Modifying your self-talk will help you remain calm and logical with even the most difficult customers.

2. Let the customer vent. Listen and don't interrupt. Chances are the customer has memorized exactly what he is going to say, so you might as well let him finish. If the customer is in a public place, try to move to a private room and deal with the situation. Don't rush this step; you'll know when the venting is finished, usually by an audible outflow of air.

One of the most important things you can do at this point is known as the POWER OF THE PEN! Take out a pen and take notes of what the customer is telling you. When you write it down, you reinforce that you are actually interested and that you plan to take action. In most every case, the upset customers will slow down, lower their voices, and stop using inappropriate language. Even if you are on the telephone—let the customer know that you are taking notes. You may also use the need to take notes as a reason to ask the customer to join you at a table where you can write more easily. This of course may remove them from a more public area where it's disruptive to other customers and coworkers.

3. Don't move to logic yet; deal with the customer's emotions first. Get your customers talking about what's upsetting them. Here are some tips:

- Show empathy for the situation. "Mr. Jones, I would be upset too if I received a $350 electric bill."
- Find areas of agreement with your customer. "How frustrating to have to call back for the second time."
- Restate what you heard them say. "So you're concerned because this is the highest bill you've ever received from us—I share your concern."
- Thank the customer (yes, thank him) for bringing the situation to your attention.

Each of these empathetic statements moves you and the customer to a point of agreement rather than disagreement. If you can guess what thoughts are in the customers' heads and what feelings are in their hearts, then you can respond empathetically by stating what it is that they are thinking or feeling. It's that easy—just turn their thoughts and feelings into your words. Remember, you are just sharing in their emotions, you are not bashing or condemning your organization.

The goal is to gradually move the customer from an emotional to a logical state of mind.

4. **Avoid emotional trigger words.** All these do are escalate the anger. Have you ever stood in line for an hour or more to renew a driver's license or register your car only to find out that you have to come back with more paperwork? Were you angry when you left? Probably so, but not because you needed more documents but because you were greeted with emotional trigger words such as, "Look lady . . ." or "It's state policy." Try using calming words and phrases instead.

Triggers	Calmers
Policy	Here's what we can do
Can't	Can
Sorry/I understand	Thank You
No, I don't know	I can find out
But	And
You should have	What others have found helpful
The only thing we can do	A good option for you is

5. **Delay action or consult a second opinion.** If all else fails, call time out. Say something like, "I want to give you the best resolution. Let me look into this matter and I'll get back with you in a few minutes." Consult with a team leader or the manager and, if necessary, bring one of them in on the conversation. Some angry customers calm down just because their grievance has been taken to a higher level. When all is said and done and the situation is resolved, the customer will remember how he was treated longer than the problem itself.

Once you have been successful in calming the customer down, you are ready to move to problem solving. The objective now is to resolve your customer's problem immediately, whether he is on the phone or standing in front of you. Here's a good approach:

- Put everything else aside and focus all of your experience and your talent on how to fix the problem.
- If possible, involve the customer in the solution by asking a question such as "What can I do to make this right?" or "How would you like for us to handle this?" You will be surprised at how reasonable the requests will be. In most cases the customer's solution will involve less than you might have offered. And since the customer thought of it, he'll be much happier and more satisfied with the outcome.
- Offer a solution based on what the customer thinks.
- Finally, give the customer your personal commitment to his or her satisfaction. Give your name, extension, and days that you work so the customer can contact you with any further questions. This both reassures the customer and gives him a person—you—who knows the history of the situation and with whom he has built some rapport.

On some occasions, no matter how hard you have tried, the situation with a customer has gone haywire and you must deliver bad news. A long-awaited special order item for a Christmas gift has been discontinued by the manufacturer. The shipment of parts to an automobile assembly plant has been delayed because of a truck breakdown. The telephone installation scheduled for this afternoon will have to be rescheduled because a thunderstorm took down some lines in another area. There are hundreds of reasons! Here, are seven suggestions on how to deliver bad news and still keep the customer in your corner.

1. Inform the customer as early as possible. You've heard the phrase, "Bad news is like a dead fish. It only gets worse with time." Most customers are understanding people, if you keep them informed in a timely manner.

2. Inform the customer over the phone or in person, not by letter or e-mail. The personal touch is critical at a time like this.

3. Get to the point quickly: "You're not going to like hearing this."

4. Treat the customer fairly. It will be remembered. Spend some time (and even money) fostering goodwill.

5. Apologize sincerely. Thank the customer for their patience and understanding.

6. Ask for another opportunity to serve them in the future.

7. Do not let it affect your interaction with the next customer.

Customer Recovery Skills

- Thank them for coming to you and hear them out with great empathy.
- Take responsibility for fixing the problem.
- Solve the problem quickly.
- Involve the customer.
- Do something extra.
- Follow up.

---

1. Thank them. Customers can tell when you are faking it! Be sincere and thank them for taking the time to come to you with this. This is a time when tone of voice and body language are all important. Use a tone and express feelings in the same manner as you would if you had been wronged.

2. Take responsibility for fixing the problem. Don't lay blame and don't make excuses, just solve the problem. Many customer-focused organizations have a policy that the associate first hearing of a problem owns it until it is resolved. That may mean getting others involved, doing some research, and then getting back to the customer with an answer.

3. Solve the problem quickly. Customers want a resolution to the problem, and they don't want to wait very long for an answer. For example, a customer calls his supplier after having received an invoice with no purchase order number included. A quick response would be, "Thank you for pointing that out. You shouldn't have been inconvenienced with this. Let me read that purchase order number to you now," or "I can e-mail or fax you a corrected invoice or put one in the mail today. Which would you prefer?" Problem solved!

4. Involve the customer. Find out what is most useful to them, not what is easiest for you. Notice in the example just given that the supplier involved the customer by asking whether he wanted the new invoice e-mailed, faxed, or sent by mail. Involving the customer is easy to do but is a skill often forgotten in service recovery.

5. Apologize at the end for the inconvenience, the disruption, or whatever the problem has caused. Then and very importantly, do something EXTRA. Correcting the problem is not enough. Recognize the "hassle factor" that your customer experienced. A gift certificate, complimentary glass of wine, or deep discounts on a price are just a few examples of little extras that don't cost much and make the difference in winning back a lost customer. Here are a few other innovative ideas:

- A dentist's office that gives movie passes to patients who have had to wait an unreasonably long time to be seen
- A fast food restaurant that gives a choice of a free order of French fries or dessert to customers who have been in line a very long time

- A department store that takes an additional percentage off the retail price when an item has to be backordered for a customer
- A copy machine repair company that brings a complimentary case of paper to a business when it has exceeded the estimated repair date and time following a trouble call

---

What Can You Do?

List below a few extras that you and your organization might offer to disappointed customers to recover their loyalty.

_____

_____

_____

_____

_____

Note to team leaders
What types of extras do you need to make available to your associates so they can recover disappointed customers? What guidelines should you give so that associates will know when to use those extras?

6. **Follow up.** Make sure the customer is satisfied. Follow-up telephone calls are particularly effective.

Scott Cook, founder of Intuit Corporation, said "If you can't please your current customers, you don't deserve new ones." Dealing effectively with angry patrons is one of the most important challenges you face in retaining and expanding your customer base.

The time needed to complete this exercise is twenty minutes for each section.

EXERCISE: Customer Service Challenges

A. Working in one or more groups, brainstorm for twenty minutes a list of the worst service experiences that you have encountered as a customer. Summarize your experiences in the box below, then indicate for each situation one of the following reasons people get angry or upset with service.

- You did not get what you expected.
- Someone was rude.
- Someone was indifferent.
- No one listened.

Summary of service experience	Reason for unsatisfactory service
1.	
2.	
3.	
4.	
5.	

B. For each situation discussed and summarized in the first part of the exercise, discuss and then list two to three ways in which the service provider could have better handled the situation or resolved the problem.

Situation (from list in Part A) **How could situation have been better handled?**

1.   1.

                                             2.

                                             3.

2.   1.

                                             2.

                                             3.

3.   1.

                                             2.

                                             3.

4.   1.

                                             2.

                                             3.

5.   1.

                                             2.

                                             3.

It's a Wrap

Did you catch all of the following points?

Why customers get upset

- ★ Broken promises and unmet expectations
- ★ Rude behavior
- ★ Indifference: "Sorry, that's our policy."
- ★ No one listened

Dealing with challenging customers

- ★ Present yourself in a calm manner; remember the S.T.O.P. factors
- ★ Let the customer vent
- ★ Deal with the emotion before trying logic
- ★ Get a second opinion
- ★ Move to problem solving

Delivering bad news

- ★ Keep customer informed
- ★ Personal touch
- ★ Get to the point
- ★ Be fair and foster goodwill
- ★ Apologize
- ★ Ask for another chance

Recovering disappointed customers

- ★ Thank them for coming to you
- ★ Take responsibility
- ★ Solve quickly
- ★ Involve customer
- ★ Do something extra
- ★ Apologize at the end (not the beginning)
- ★ Follow up and through

Chapter Ten

Customer Feedback: Are You Hungry?

There is only one rule here. The customer defines your service. Did you get that? The customer DEFINES your service! It sounds simple, logical. Then why do so many service providers operate as if *they* define the service? Why do they fail to ask the simple questions, "How are we doing?" "Are you pleased with our products and/or services?" "What else can we do for you?" "Will you come back to see us again?" And, the most significant question, "Would you refer a friend or family member to our business?"

I have talked to countless business owners, executives, and frontline associates who say, "We have a good feel for our customers. We just

don't get that many calls, letters, or comments. And management sees every one we do get so that we can keep in touch." Keep in touch! Give me a break. That's like waiting for a plant to die in order to say, "I guess it needed water."

Numerous studies over the last several years have reported consistently that only 2 to 5 percent (depending on your industry) of your customers complain voluntarily. This is not 2 to 5 percent of your total customer base. This is 2 to 5 percent of the unhappy customers, the "I had an unsatisfactory (I may not return) experience" customers. So for every letter or phone call you receive from an unhappy customer, picture another ninety-six walking out without saying a word.

In today's busy, demand-upon-demand kind of world, you have to actively solicit your customers' impressions (the good and bad). And you must do it in a creative, nonintrusive, easy-to-obtain way. Once you have the feedback, you must do something with it. Not next quarter, next year, or next decade, but now.

A good guide to follow is the A, B, C, D method:

A sk for feedback

B elieve what they're telling you

C ommunicate your results

D o something with what you've learned

A = Ask for Feedback

Asking for customer feedback may be formal or informal. It can be in person, by mail, by phone, by e-mail, or by website. It can be conversational or statistical. What's important is that you seek it.

The hotel industry is skilled at getting feedback. One major urban hotel has a program called Elevator Ears. That pretty much says it. At this hotel, employees are riding up and down the elevators all day long with customers. In fact, they are encouraged to do so. But these employees are trained not to think of the elevator as a way of getting from floor 2 to floor 12. They are trained to think of it as an opportunity to hear from their guests. It's an amazingly simple way to gather information from a somewhat captured audience. And you hear it all: guests who just registered, a couple from the restaurant, a businesswoman from the seminar, a golfer, a swimmer, and maybe even a late sleeper. The fact is, these are the people using the hotel services, and they often have comments. Many times these comments are volunteered without asking. Haven't you taken that moment of reflection in an elevator to say, "Boy, am I ready to get to the room. I thought we'd never get checked in." or "I guess that waitress was having a bad day." Or perhaps you've made a comment on the parking garage or the smell of smoke in the hallways.

Employees at this hotel are also trained to initiate a conversation if they do not hear one. "How is everyone this morning? I hope you're enjoying your stay at our hotel." And if that doesn't kick it off, the employee may add, "Has anyone tried our restaurant this morning?" or "I see you've been to the health club, how did you find our services there?" Can you just imagine the impression this makes!

W Hotels, Starwood's chic hotel brand, also has coached its employees to listen for clues that will help anticipate guests' needs. Complain to your husband on your cell phone about a sore throat while you're standing at the check-in desk, and W employees might send up a cup of chicken soup gratis.

One of the things I like best about the Elevator Ears program is that it's not just for hotels. You can take the same principles of employee training for feedback and apply them to hospitals, retail stores, banks, and even doctors' offices. It's a matter of training employees to listen and to report. Can you think of listening posts for your business? A listening post can be any location where easy dialogue can take place—hallways, waiting rooms, around counters, throughout restaurants, most any public place.

Name three "listening posts" in your organization.

1. _____

2. _____

3. _____

As a team, can you determine a simple but effective way to share comments from your listening post? Suggestion: Give each team member the challenge of recording three observations in a week and then set aside ten minutes at a team meeting to share the observations. Develop a simple table, and keep a record of the types of comments that you hear. This will help you track any problem areas or items needing attention.

So Who's Asking Whom?

Let's talk a moment about whom we survey for service feedback. Is it:

- the purchaser of our product or service?
- family or friends of the purchaser?

- the end user of our product or service?
- a former or "lost" customer?
- our vendors/suppliers?
- our employees?

A hospital illustrates how difficult it can be to define your customer. The most obvious customer in a hospital is the patient. And certainly the patient is important. But did the patient admit himself/herself, or did a doctor direct them to the hospital? Oh, so the doctor is really the important customer. Did the doctor choose the hospital based on services, or was he or she directed by the insurance provider? I see, so now it's the insurance provider. Did the doctor have several choices, and did the physician's staff have influence regarding the hospital they work best with? Did the patient's employer select the health plan, and how did they choose participating hospitals and physicians in their plan? It gets complex doesn't it?

One of the forgotten groups of customers to survey is those who once did business with you but are now doing business with the competition. What made them leave? What is the competition doing better? Is there a way to recover their business? By surveying this group of folks you not only learn a great deal about your service potholes, but your last message to the former customer is that you care! Wouldn't you prefer that this follow-up be the last impression with the customer as opposed to the bitter taste they carry from the poor service that drove them away?

Note to team leader

An automobile service shop trained its driver for the shuttle bus to solicit questions and debrief customers. "What do you think of our service shop? How friendly were the folks taking your order? Would you recommend us to your friends and neighbors?" Think for a moment. Have you adequately trained everyone who has contact with your customers?

Another effective feedback method involves the use of "lost job" questionnaires. These questionnaires are sent to prospective customers. They are especially useful for companies involved with contracting bids and technical proposals. I remember an article in *Inc.* magazine years ago that featured T&K Roofing, a contractor in Iowa who used a very effective lost job survey. Many companies believe that they lose bids based solely on price. T&K discovered this not to be true. They found that many of their bids were lost due to other reasons such as follow-through, sales rep inexperience, or lack of knowledge. They gained great insight from their surveys, which helped them to grow despite eight new competitors in their marketplace. Following is the T&K survey questionnaire:

T&K Roofing Company Inc.

At T&K Roofing Company, our number one priority is to provide and deliver goods and services that our clients want and value. By completing this evaluation, you will assist us in assessing why we did not meet your requirements.

Please identify the following items that affected your decision NOT to accept our bid. Please feel free to be completely honest. Your feedback is very important to us, and your responses will remain confidential.

Thank you for your assistance,

Thomas M. Tjelmeland, President

Were any of the following a major factor in your decision NOT to award the contract to T&K?

1.	Price	Yes	No
2.	T&K reputation (integrity)	Yes	No
3.	Service Offerings	Yes	No
4.	Available warranty	Yes	No
5.	T&K location	Yes	No
6.	Project schedule	Yes	No
7.	Roof system requirements	Yes	No

8. Billing terms   Yes   No
9. Established relationship with another contractor   Yes   No
10. Please list the main reasons T&K was not selected:
11. (optional) Can you tell us who was awarded the contract?
12. If price was the reason for losing the business, can you tell us by what percentage T&K was higher than the selected contractor?
13. If service offerings and/or capabilities affected the selection, what did T&K not offer that the competition did?
14. If your project is rebid at a later date, would you like us to contact you again? When?

Please rate the effectiveness of the presentation made by our sales representative (1 = lowest rating, 10 = highest rating). This information will be kept confidential from the representative.

15. Receptiveness and understanding of the project   1 2 3 4 5 6 7 8 9 10
    requirements and the needs of your firm.
16. Presentation of T&K Roofing's capabilities,   1 2 3 4 5 6 7 8 9 10
    products, service offerings, and recognitions.
18. Willingness and ability to answer all of   1 2 3 4 5 6 7 8 9 10
    your questions.
19. Professional appearance.   1 2 3 4 5 6 7 8 9 10
20. Demonstrated respect for the competition.   1 2 3 4 5 6 7 8 9 10
21. Timeliness or response time of initial contact   1 2 3 4 5 6 7 8 9 10
    until bid presentation.
22. How many times after the representative   1 2 3 4 5 6 7 8 9 10
    submitted his quote did he call to see if you
    had any additional questions?
23. Comments/Questions:

We have discussed a number of people you can ask about your service, but now back to you, the employee. Don't you know a great deal about the customer care being provided in your organization? As a frontline associate who works with customers all day long, you should have a comment or two. When were you last asked to provide input on service delivery?

Every organization has a myriad of customers and people who influence customer choice. A simple annual survey to a primary base of customers and employees is hardly enough, not if you want to truly understand what your customers like and don't like about what you do.

The Best Way to Ask

Companies often wonder how best to survey their customers. The answer is somewhat dependent on your company size, the nature of your business, the frequency of your customer interaction, and the depth of information that you are attempting to gather. Customer feedback is usually grouped into one of two categories: quantitative and qualitative.

Quantitative information is that which is of sufficient volume that it has statistical validity. In other words, you can rely on the accuracy of the responses to be a reflection of your total customer base, and you can feel confident in making decisions based on the data provided. As an example, if your quantitative research shows that 89 percent of your customers do not like your automated voice mail system, then you should consider changing it.

Qualitative information is not statistically valid and should be used with caution. It does not project customer trends and behaviors. Some of the best qualitative surveying is done face-to-face by asking the customers about their experience. Imagine the wealth of feedback if a grocery store manager made a point of asking ten customers a day about their shopping experience. We're not talking about questions like, "How was your shopping experience with us today?" That's much too vague, open-ended, and it doesn't invite conversation. In fact, it invites a simple "fine" when things weren't fine. Think if the store manager introduced herself and said, "I hope we are stocking everything you wanted. Were we out of any particular items or did you have trouble locating them?" Many questions could be asked, but they should be specific, conversational, and easy to answer.

Another popular qualitative research method is mystery shopping. Mystery shoppers are paid to interact with service providers for the purposes of evaluating their performance such as service response time, attitude, and product/service knowledge. They also look at other service attributes such as facility appearance, cleanliness, and signage.

Other qualitative surveying techniques, such as focus groups, are often used to test new ideas, products, or even research questionnaires before they are applied to significant numbers. Your opportunities for qualitative feedback are endless. You should also try customer feedback forums. These are like customer councils. Bring eight to twelve of your customers together and converse with them about your products and services. Feed or entertain them and most are more than happy to share their thoughts. A simpler idea is to invite customers into one of your company meetings. Ask them to share a little about their businesses and how they perceive your services. Employees love this kind of interaction, and it allows them to put a face and personality with a customer. Customers enjoy the relationship building as well.

Feedback Tools: A Few Examples

Quantitative

- Telephone surveys
- Mailed questionnaires
- Business reply cards (counter top or product insert)
- Personal interviews
- Touch-tone phone surveys at call centers
- Internet questionnaires

Qualitative

- Focus groups/customer forums
- Internet chat lines
- Mystery shoppers and teleshoppers
- Employee observations

Quantitative research is an art and a science, and we recommend that it be outsourced to professionals. First, outside researchers can provide an anonymous and independent voice to your customer. This often helps the customers feel more at ease in being totally candid in their response. Secondly, the research professionals will construct survey tools that do not bias the customer responses with wording that is confusing or leading. Thirdly, the researchers can perform analysis of the data and make recommendations that in-house resources usually aren't equipped to do.

Most importantly, do not overlook the various ways in which research can be conducted. With the Internet explosion, many companies are using websites and targeted e-mails to gain customer feedback. Several new Internet service companies have sprung up that solicit online consumer complaints then make that data available to companies and industries. Other companies find that automated phone surveys work for them. Of course, mailed questionnaires, business reply cards, product or bill inserts, and phone surveys are always options.

Many businesses such as hotels, airlines, hospitals, restaurants, and movie theaters have their customers "captured" for a period of time. This can be a great time to access information about the services provided. It's timely and shows that you care.

Deliver It

Deliver It is a great campaign that is conducted at Wachovia Bank. I like it because it maximizes employee involvement and interest in customer care. The name, *Deliver It*, does not refer to delivering service as you might expect. It refers to delivering The Promise. The Promise is an oath or cultural code that all employees are expected to know and embrace. It's their way of doing business.

Deliver It is a huge program that requires commitment. It entails training over a three-month period, and it requires active participation by the employees. The program is effective because it:

- reinforces the bank's Seven Steps to Exceptional Customer Service;
- trains Wachovia employees to be their own mystery shoppers— for the bank's own customer contact personnel, and for other retail operations;
- serves not only as an effective reporting system for service deficiencies, it has a recognition component for outstanding performance as well.

Think about it. As a frontline customer care associate, how better to focus on the attributes of exceptional service than to be continually looking for them in the actions of others? And you have to admit it, for most of us, there is something fun about mystery shopping. It's like being an undercover detective. By mystery shopping other retail operations, you get some fresh examples of clueless, complacent (and yes, sometimes exceptional) service to take back and share with your associates.

The survey tools used in the *Deliver It* program are excellent. They ask specific questions about the transaction taking place. For example, for a telephone mystery shop, the transaction asks, "If you were placed on hold, did the employee ask permission?" and "How long was the hold?" Each answer is given a numerical rating such that total scores can be quantified. This allows rankings to be assigned at the branch bank level and serves as the basis for individual and branch rewards!

Another program similar to *Deliver It* is used by a large Parks and Recreation Commission for their numerous park sites and activities. In their newsletters to park members, they ask for volunteers to serve as mystery shoppers to help evaluate the quality of their services. Additionally, park employees can sign up for the program to mystery shop activities outside their own area. Incentives are offered with free passes to special programs, and the response is wonderful. The volunteers are brought together for initial training and then sent to the field. Some critics may say that these types of in-house programs are not advisable. After all, the mystery shoppers are not trained professionals. But we are all consumers, and with proper selection and training, the benefits of employee (and membership) involvement far outweigh the potential concerns.

Allow fifteen minutes to complete design of Mystery Shop form. Allow fifteen minutes in team meetings for Story Telling.

Exercise: I've Got Your Number

A. Using the following template, design your own mystery shop form. Make it a simple form that relates to the type of business you do. Substitute any service attributes that are key to the care you provide your customers.

Mystery Shop: I've Got Your Number

Shopper Name: _____ Date:_____
Business Name: _____

1. Was I greeted in a warm and welcoming way   Y / N / NA
   that made me feel special?
2. Did the employee introduce himself/herself?   Y / N / NA
3. After telling the employee my name,   Y / N / NA
   did he/she use my name?
4. Did the employee listen well to what I needed?   Y / N / NA
5. Was the employee knowledgeable about   Y / N / NA
   the products/services?
6. Did the employee use good eye contact?   Y / N / NA
7. Was the appearance of the employee   Y / N / NA
   professional/appropriate?
8. Did his/her body language indicate   Y / N / NA
   enthusiasm and interest?
9. Was the employee's tone sincere/empathetic/   Y / N / NA
   professional?
10. Did the employee add to your service experience?   Y / N / NA
11. Did you feel valued as a customer?   Y / N / NA
12. Would you recommend this employee for   Y / N / NA
    hire to your business?

Overall, rate your satisfaction with this employee.

1	2	3	4	5	6	7	8	9	10
YUCK			EH			OK			WOW

Notes/Comments: _____

_____

B. Set a goal for three to five contacts per week in which you will use your Mystery Shop form to evaluate the service of others. If you primarily deal with customers by telephone, then shop those types of businesses. It is helpful to pick businesses that are in a similar business or in direct competition with yours.

Be prepared to talk about your interactions at your next team meeting. Rotate the mystery shopper among all team members, or have all participate and randomly pick those to "story tell" about their experience. Don't forget to relate the lessons learned for the improvement of your own service.

C. Among your team members, complete the following:

If there is one thing I'd like to see the company improve on, it would be:

_____

_____

_____

_____

_____

A final comment on customer surveys. If you decide to use written questionnaires or comment cards of any kind, be sure to have postage paid. It is a rule not to be broken: if you want feedback, make it easy for your customers to give it.

B = Believe What They Are Telling You

Why wouldn't we believe our customers? We have taken the time to ask for their opinions, of course we'll listen to what they say.

As a loyal and committed employee, we often find it hard to take criticism about our businesses. We either don't really listen to what the customers are telling us, or just as bad, we begin to justify our position and place blame elsewhere. Imagine for a moment that you are in a manufacturing plant that supplies plastic products for the auto industry. You have just conducted a customer satisfaction survey and learned that your customers are receiving an abnormally high number of shipments with cracked plastic parts.

Your response: "Well, they left here just fine. What are THEY doing with them once the parts arrive?" Or, "They were okay when we loaded them on the truck. I wouldn't doubt that they were damaged in shipment. I've seen how those truck drivers handle them. The customer just needs to file an insurance claim." In any case, the customer has not been helped. It's a poor way of saying, "We've done our job—it's in your hands now." This type of thinking will soon lead to customer defection. It is a narrow way of viewing the customer experience. The customer's experience begins when you or your company are first contacted, and it continues until the product is in use and has been paid for. In fact, the experience goes beyond that to include service after the sale, advertising reinforcement, warranties, and right on until the next purchase is made. It's a complete cycle that should not be broken by lack of attention to a problem.

Recently I worked with a retailer that was in denial about its role. This store was very diligent about seeking customer feedback. Historically, they had done quite well in their service measurements, but an undesirable trend began with the decline in the perceptions of the frontline staff. Reports were coming back monthly showing that the sales and service staffs were no longer being perceived as "helpful, friendly, or even professional." The retailer remarked, "Well, that's not altogether surprising with the unemployment ratios we're facing in this area. Heck, we're lucky just to have warm bodies that can take the money and provide the correct change." No wonder the store was getting feedback like this on its surveys. Instead of investing in the training and motivation, instead of reviewing how the recruitment and retention practices are being revamped in light of the low unemployment, this store was excusing the problem.

Here are some other common phrases heard that should sound the alarms:

- "We all know that only the disgruntled customers take time to complete the surveys."
- "I'm not so sure this isn't just a fluke in the reporting this month. Let's wait until next month's report to see what it says."
- "The way the questions are phrased, it invites complaints."
- "What do these customers expect anyway? Nobody is going to make these guys happy."

Whatever the issue, if it's affecting overall customer care, it shouldn't be passed off with excuses. And whether you are part of management or a member of the all-important frontline, you can have an impact on the situation. But nothing will happen if you don't believe the results in the first place.

A new way of measuring customer satisfaction developed by Fred Reichheld makes it very easy to "believe what they are telling you." Called the Net Promoter Score, this method makes use of the most powerful question you can ask a customer: "Would you recommend us to a friend or colleague?" Reichheld classifies customers, based on their responses to this question on a 10-point scale, either as promoters (9–10), passives (7–8), or detractors (0–6). The "net promoter score" is simply your percentage of detractors subtracted from your percentage of promoters. For more information on this powerful tool, go to *www. netpromoter.com.*

C = Communicate Your Results

Too often, organizations gather this type of customer feedback, and then they fail to share it. It gets hidden away in some management closet. This type of information needs to be shared, and shared creatively!

Not every audience is appropriate for the information gathered, but you should go through a checklist of who could benefit from the information. Take, for example, some very positive results from either a quantitative or qualitative survey. Think how this could be built into your client communications (newsletters, report letters, brochure materials, website, shopping bags, etc.). Imagine how powerful it could be as part of your recruitment and training materials for Human Resources. Just imagine that you are interviewing for a position at a new company and they roll out some strong customer satisfaction statistics, or maybe some testimonials from customers. Wouldn't you feel better about the company and your potential for enjoying the work there? Strong positive endorsements can serve as wonderful reinforcement messages that current clients are making a good decision. Likewise, they are effective morale boosters for staff in all departments. Use the information at team meetings, company meetings, and special event gatherings. Some companies have even printed great results of testimonials on T-shirts, coffee mugs, and other specialty items.

So it's fun to think of ways to use the good comments, but what about the not so good? These need to be shared as well, but with a little more caution and tact. Customers want to know that they've been heard. Individual letters to disgruntled customers can be very effective. Thank them for their input; you have no way of improving without it. It lets them know that you are listening, and that you have plans to address the situation. Customers will tend to have more faith in your commitment to turn things around when you are honest in sharing deficiencies.

At Ben & Jerry's ice cream company, they have incredibly effective letters to customers (you'll enjoy this story). A customer, who was seven months pregnant, had a midnight craving for Chunky Monkey ice cream. She managed to persuade her husband to brave a blinding snowstorm for a pint. Upon scooping the ice cream into a bowl, she was disappointed at the sparseness of walnuts in the product. From past experience she was accustomed to many more. She wrote the company and complained. The letter responding to her situation was great! First, the company apologized to her for the "wimpy, anemic, under-chunked pint." What's more, they included a coupon for a free pint because, as the letter stated, "you have to feed that baby." Score! They just created a customer experience.

D = Do Something with What You've Learned

Sounds like a kindergarten message, doesn't it? It is fairly basic, but it is so often ignored. Make sure that delivering the customer experience is one of your priorities. This doesn't mean that you have to address every issue ever raised by a customer. Sort out the priority problem areas and begin a plan of attack. Your time, energy, and, yes, sometimes money, are investments that will reap great rewards.

One company that's particularly adept at listening to its customers and then delivering what they want is Superquinn, the Irish grocery chain. Founder and President Feargal Quinn walks each of his stores' aisles every month, talking to customers. Twice monthly, he invites twelve customers to join him for a two-hour roundtable discussion. He asks them about service levels, pricing, cleanliness, product quality, new product lines, recent displays, advertising promotions and so on; he also asks what items they still buy from his competitors and why. Quinn uses what he learns to evaluate store managers and continually improve the company's strategy and its execution of that strategy.

For example, Quinn once learned that 25 percent of Superquinn shoppers were not buying from the store bakeries. When he made bakery managers and employees aware of this statistic and began tracking it, they came up with scores of creative ideas to build traffic. Customers soon were enticed to visit the bakery by the aroma of freshly made doughnuts; once there, they found baskets of warm samples. Today, more than 90 percent of customers buy at least one item from the bakery every week.

What's more, Superquinns awards its customers "goof points" for pointing out things like out-of stock items, a dirty floor, or a checkout line longer than three people. These goof points are good for discounts off future purchases. Now that's customer involvement!!

Note to team leader

In many instances the responsibility to do something regarding poor customer responses is a management issue. If left in the hands of the frontline, they'd surely take action. It may be because management is more removed from the customer that they traditionally don't act as quickly. They don't see the pain as clearly. Think about it. How can you make sure that action is taken where appropriate?

It's a Wrap

Did you catch all of the following points?

Feedback: Ask and you shall receive!

- ★ Some conventional and unconventional methods
  - Surveys
  - Hotline
  - Follow-up letters
  - Employees listen for comments
- ★ Don't forget to survey lost customers
- ★ Quantitative vs. qualitative methods

Feedback: Believe what they are telling you

- ★ Don't dismiss criticism
- ★ Don't place blame elsewhere
- ★ Do listen for phrases that sound the "defensive alarm"

Feedback: Communicate your results

- ★ Share the data—good and bad
- ★ Make it fun!

Feedback: Do something with what you've learned

Chapter Eleven

Technology and E-commerce: Enhancer or Inhibitor

It is dangerous in today's world to write about topics such as technology and e-commerce. Why? At the rate that these areas are advancing, the information we give you may well be out-of-date by the time our words meet the press. On the other hand, that's actually one of the beauties of technology. It can be exciting, scary, complex, rapid, confusing, simplifying, and (to most of us) a complete mystery all at once.

As we discuss technology and e-commerce, we want you to look beyond the gadget-of-the-day and look at technology's impact from the perspective of the customer. How is technology enhancing or inhibiting the customer experience?

I was reading a copy of *Down East* (the magazine of the state of Maine) when I came across a wonderful note from one of their readers:

"I believe many people desperately want to retain a simple world, a caring world, and whether we are crazy or bitter or reckless or moody, or are born an outsider, we are all seeking the great gift of contentment, the one perfect, never-to-be forgotten gift that I doubt will ever be bestowed by a computer."

Can't you identify with this? Don't get me wrong—I have my own love-hate relationship with my laptop, BlackBerry, voice mail, e-mail, faxes, DirectTV, websites, ATMs, cell phones, scanners, digital cameras, security systems, pagers, and the innumerable trappings of our sophisticated/automated/electronically translated world. There are days when I covet my hardware and software niceties, and then there are those other times. Fact is, advances in technology are here to stay, and it's our challenge to make human use of them.

Being There, Electronically of Course

While watching a morning news show, I was struck by a story of an innovative company and their use of the Internet. Before talking about their product, let's first describe the customer and her need.

The need: You are the parent of an eleven-month-old girl. She is your first child. Each day you drop off your child at the day care and drive to work with a blanket of guilt. And when guilt is not there, then sadness takes its place. You miss seeing your little girl at play, watching her toddle, watching her sleep. Day in and day out, you somehow deal with it.

The solution: a website "see you" cam. For a small fee you can access the web, enter your pass code, and have instant access to a live video telecast from your child's day care. Wow! While it will never replace being there, what a miracle of technology. And on the newscast—parents, day care workers, even employers—all were interviewed for their reactions to this creative application of technology. Each person interviewed spoke of the benefits—the comfort, the security, and all the tangibles and intangibles of such a service.

Imagine the uses of this same web video service in hospitals, nursing homes, and home health agencies. Does it have its downsides and its detractors? Sure. However, it is still a great example of a creative use of technology to enhance customer service.

One of the more creative and human uses of technology that we've seen is by Jansport, a leading manufacturer of outdoor supplies such as the ever-popular backpack. Not only do we love this company for their quality products and their lifetime guarantees, but most of all because they have a personal service culture.

The eleven-year-old son of a friend of mine has had one of their backpacks for years. It's been battered about in lockers, lunchrooms, sand, surf, and sludge. As life took its toll, the zipper finally broke. In a mailer (provided by the company) the young man's father sent off this well-worn backpack to be repaired—at no charge I might add. Within a week he received the following post card in the mail—addressed directly to his son:

> Hi!
>
> It's me, your favorite Back Pack. Warranty Service Camp is really cool. The other packs are really different, and I love my pack counselor. I miss hanging out with you and carrying your gear all the time. I can't wait to see you. They say they're sending me home soon. Gotta run . . . we're doing zipper races today.
>
> Little Pack
>
> P.S. If you need to reach me, my numbers are on the other side of this card.

Consider what Jansport has just done. In a very personal, human-touch way, they have used technology to communicate their service while building a heck of a bond with the customer. They knew the pack's owner by name. I'm sure their database tells them how long he's had the pack, how old he is, and most likely what some of his interests are. After all, they could have just sent a card that said they had received the product and it was due for return by XX date. Many companies don't even bother with that level of communication. But Jansport chose to innovatively apply their technology to provide a personal level of service. And they didn't stop there. When the backpack was returned, it had another post card enclosed.

Hi,

I'm your pack's counselor, Big J. S. We really enjoyed getting to know little J. S. at Warranty Service Camp this year—what a star! A strapping little rascal, your pack led the pack in bug smashing, carrying ghost stories, and as you know, Little J. S. made quite a showing in the zipper races.

We know you must have missed the little bagger like crazy. You'll be pleased to know that we worked out those little problems that you told us about, so your pack is back to full zip strength.

Every happiness,

Big J. S.

Obviously, these notes were computer generated. And note the language: "zipper races, zip strength" and all the references to back packs. They must have countless form letters in their database that tailor the note to the receiver. It certainly shows that they know the product, the problem, the customer, and how to serve!

A Walk on the Uglier Side

Contrast this with a call I made recently to my laptop computer manufacturer's help desk. After what seemed to be an endless journey through their website, a fruitless effort to pinpoint my specific problem, I finally abandoned the web and sought the comfort of the twenty-four-hour help desk at 12:30 A.M. As expected, I was connected directly into an automated phone system. For my appetizer, I was presented with four choices of buttons to push. My entree menu included no less than eight alternatives. My dessert was another six, and my fourth menu—oh, I don't even recall. Finally, for the first time apparent to me, I could actually push 0 for a real live person. I had now been on the phone for almost twenty minutes when Tom answered and attempted to clarify that I am with the U.S. military. "No," I told him, at which point he stated that he couldn't help me, and I must call back for their residential customer service. "Please, NO!" I implored, not wanting to go through their automated maze again. Unfortunately, I had no other option. Tom couldn't access my records, nor could he transfer me to the correct department. At least that was his claim. As the clock ticked toward 2 A.M., I abandoned the call and slumped off to bed. How I longed to just call and reach a friendly person who empathized with my need and could assure me of a solution. Strike three, I was out.

Here's one more great story from the dark side of technology. In a letter to the late syndicated newspaper columnist Ann Landers, a poor "customer" related being hounded by the billing department of the local department of education about a student loan. The wacky thing was that the billing department admitted that the correct loan balance was $0.00. The problem was that the computer had no way of deleting this balance from its accounts receivable without receiving a check. In order to stop the harassment of monthly collection letters, this dutiful customer sent in a check for $0. She found that calling the customer service center was useless because "they don't always communicate with the billing department." Happy ending? The collection efforts did stop, but the craziest thing of all was that the billing department did try to cash the $0 check!

Unfortunately, the above situations are becoming the norm. Ever tally how many calls you make to businesses in a day that are actually answered by a live person within five (we think that's reasonable) rings? If you track it for a while, you will find that percentage to be pretty low.

Allow fifteen minutes to complete the following tables.

EXERCISE: Person to Person

Select five places of business to call. They could be your competition, one of your suppliers, or just a pick from the telephone directory. Note how the call was received and any comments you may have. Share these with your service team and discuss how people perceive calls into your business or department.

Name/Type of Business	# rings	L = live P = in person	Comments

It Can Be the Simple Things, Even with Technology

Sometimes the word "technology" conjures up images of satellite transmissions, bytes, and strange programmer types to make it all work.

What's silly is that most of us don't take advantage of the simplest offerings of today's technology—offerings that benefit the customer.

It's hard to imagine that at some point you haven't called Pizza Hut for a home delivery. Because they automatically recognize your phone number, they may say, "Oh Miss Jones, would you like the same pizza you ordered last time? A large, thin crust pepperoni and mushroom?" It's become second nature to many of us now, but do you remember how impressed you were the first time it happened? They not only knew your last order, they knew how to find your house—the directions are now in their system. So what else might they know about you? I'll give you a hint: don't ask them how much you spent on pizza in the last year. They can tell you that too, and you don't want to know.

Here's another example of a simple phone system helper. If you call Great American Business Products out of Houston, Texas, it's unlikely that you will be placed on hold. Their statistics show they answer calls within an average of twenty seconds. Should you happen to have to hold, on one of those inevitable busy days, then you will hear a recording. The message says, "Because you're on hold, we want to give you a bonus item for holding. When the representative comes on the line, please ask what your bonus item will be." A free gift—don't get that much, do you? Great American Business Products sells office supply items. So you might get a free box of pens or note pads. This small gesture catches the callers' attention and lets them know that they are valued.

When I think of large call centers, I also appreciate the occasional ones that give me an estimate of how long I can expect to be on hold. As customers, we have become so accustomed to holding that by telling us how long we can expect to wait we are somehow grateful. It allows us the option to continue holding or to call back later. It puts a little bit of control into our hands. For example, when I'm in the office, I often choose to put a call on the speakerphone, and I continue working while waiting for a representative. Furthermore, most call centers have peak hours. I appreciate the hold message telling me hours that are more accessible. I may not always have the choice to call at another time, but if I do it's my option.

So how is your phone answered at work? Has your business, like so many, gone to automated voice systems? Is the system customer friendly? What messages do you have for people on hold? Once the customer is on the line, how much information do you already know about them and their history with your company? Do you use the information that you have readily available to reinforce your relationship with the customer? So much can be done in this simple area, yet so many ignore the potential.

E-commerce and E-service— They Can Be One and the Same

If you're not already part of the e-world, it's time to wave the white flag. It's an instant access, twenty-four-hour, seven-day a week way to do business. Who wouldn't jump at it? Isn't that a large part of the service equation, not to mention the worldwide exposure that e-commerce provides from a sales and marketing perspective?

Consider the following facts gathered by Plunkett Research, Ltd.:

- Worldwide, over 1.3 billion people use the Internet.
- Over 90 million American homes and businesses have broadband access.
- Seventy-two percent of American adults surf the web regularly.
- Online advertising expenditures in 2007 were $26 billion and in 2008 accounted for 10 percent of all ad expenditures in the U.S.
- Retail items and travel purchased online in 2008 were close to $250 billion in the U.S. alone!

The impacts to our lives as consumers—and to our lives as business professionals—are limited only by our vision. Some of the conveniences that technology offers (yet is still being incorporated into our daily lives!) include:

- Your handheld computer is tracking the satellite positioning of your child's school bus so you know where it is and when to expect its arrival.

- Better yet, this same unit is tracking the whereabouts of your teenager as he drives your new car. You can know the exact locations he visited, the speed he traveled, and just when he'll walk through your door (after curfew, of course).

- Your cellular telephone "talks to" a vending machine, allowing you to purchase a soda, stamps, or a newspaper without paying cash. Known as m-commerce, technology is available that allows you to shop and pay bills using your cell phone.

- As you head for an appointment, don't worry about traffic delays. No waiting for the report from SkyChopper II. You'll have real-time access to all road conditions for your route. Some automobile manufacturers are now offering, as an option, navigational consoles that provide maps and specific directions at the push of a button (keep your eyes on the road).

- Grocery shopping—who has time? Your refrigerator will scan all contents and send electronic orders to your food/supply distribution center for delivery. Furthermore, this smart fridge will suggest recipes that can be made with the contents available.

- You are paying all your bills electronically. Your home and business mailboxes are no longer cluttered with all that unnecessary paper as invoices will come electronically as well.

- Airlines will send a real-time notification to your mobile phone, pager, or computer if a flight is running late. They will even tell you about traffic delays coming into or from your designated airport.

- Think of the fun at family reunions. No more missed relatives due to lengthy travel. Keep in touch with web cams.

Another creative use of web technology is starting to take hold. It's called computer telephony. It's relatively inexpensive software that allows talking over the Internet. Sadly it is used more in Internet gaming than it is as a service tool for business. This brings a personalization and humanization into the website world. It's a helping hand for the "I'm lost on your website" customer, and it provides an opportunity for assisting those with more specialized needs that aren't often accommodated in general web browsing. Many home and office computers now have the power and software to conduct business this way.

Taking this a step further, Hartness Technologies in Greenville, SC, has developed a new twist on "same day service." They now promote "minutes-later service." They developed a VRS (Video Response System) connecting wireless cameras and high-resolution monitors that provide live feeds for businesses and their customers in need of interactive repairs or problem solving. It's more than just video conferencing—it is the next best thing to being there with an instructional capability that saves service technicians travel time and expense. Companies like Coca Cola, Chrysler, and Hewlett Packard are seeing the benefits.

We have seen increasing numbers as well as creative uses for highly inviting touch screens in retail and travel-related businesses. It's great for hospitals, libraries, museums, and certain restaurants. Heck, Disney World has had touch screens in its park for years. Do your products have options that the customers might like to customize? How could this type of technology benefit your clientele? How might it benefit you as well?

Lands' End created a "Personal Model." This feature allows women to input their personal dimensions into the site, and a model is created for them that can then try on clothes. And taking this one step further, a company in London has created a camera booth that takes your picture from numerous angles to create a computer-transferable image for you. This photographic cloning allows you to put yourself into the world wide web as a virtual customer extraordinaire.

Whether it's retail, entertainment, health care, real estate, or politics, almost every industry is learning how to take advantage of a fuller customer experience through the Internet. Check out what your competition is doing, and see if you can one-up them with technology.

Protecting and Projecting Your E-mage

The first websites were designed by techie people, people who often didn't focus on the service elements. Many of these early sites were (and are) nothing but electronic brochures for an organization. Flat websites are not interactive, not communicative, and often not even up-to-date. They don't invite a customer in, and they don't engage them once online. For a website to be effective, it should be one of many extensions of your business. It should have the look, feel, and quality image that are consistent with your organization. It should offer easy, direct access for customers to ask questions as well as give comments. Here are some general considerations:

- Does your website design reflect your image? Is it busy or clean? Is it colorful, trendy, and techie, or warm, soft, and understated?
- Can browsers easily contact you? Do you have proper response support?
- Is your site updated regularly? Does it have opportunities for the customer to interact?
- Do you ask the customer questions about their perceptions/satisfaction with the services or products you offer?
- Do you have customer chat rooms where instant dialogue can take place with your organization or other customers?
- How quickly are e-mail inquiries responded to?
- Do you send e-mails to confirm an order, as well as when it's been shipped? Do you ask the customers about their hobbies, interests, birthdays, or any other key profile-type questions?
- Do you help direct them to related sites, offer repair advice or creative uses of your products?
- Do you assure them of security and site integrity when information is being gathered?

Allow fifteen minutes to complete the following tables.

EXERCISE: E-magine the Possibilities

As a team, brainstorm ideas that could most improve your phone system and/or your website. Name at least six to ten ideas. Take a vote and rank them in order of your top three suggestions.

Improving Service Through Technology Suggestions

1.

2.

3.

Don't just let these ideas collect dust. Do two things with this information. First, start researching what resources would be needed to implement the above ideas. Try and come up with some basic cost estimates and identify who is needed to assist with implementation. Secondly, submit this information to your management with your thoughts on why these technology enhancements would benefit the customers and/or the organization.

Don't Let Your Technology Byte You

Businesses commonly make the mistake of upgrading technology without providing support behind it. By support we are talking about the training, the staffing, and whatever components are necessary to make best use of the respective technology. To think of it in the simplest of terms, it would be comparable to a bank opening a new ATM site that is always out of money. You must not forget that when a service is offered, customers expect it to work.

One thing is certain about our tech-based customers—they can walk even faster off a website than out of your door. Their access to the competition is just a click away. No more parking headaches or time invested in the drive to your business. Imagine the loyalty it takes to keep the customer from simply clicking you to oblivion! True market leaders know that the total customer experience is what will differentiate their product or service from all the rest in today's highly competitive world.

Remember that current and emerging technology, no matter how fast, sophisticated, accurate, or cost-efficient, is still dependent on people for its success. The term "high-tech, high touch" applies to the world of customer care today and in the future. Your challenge is to use technology to enhance service levels, not to let it inhibit giving exceptional customer service.

It's a Wrap

Did you catch all of the following points?

Some creative uses of technology in customer service

Some not-so-creative applications of technology

Use of technology doesn't have to be "rocket science"

- ★ *Pizza Hut*—recording customer preferences
- ★ *Great American Business Products*—"hold for your free gift"
- ★ "Your estimated hold time is"

E-commerce and e-service—one and the same?

- ★ Internet usage is exploding—1.3 billion people worldwide
- ★ E-Business is Big Business—$250 billion in retail and travel sold online in 2008
- ★ E-magining today's technology
  - Track your child/teenager by computer
  - The refrigerator that refills itself
  - Shop and pay bills using your cell phone
  - Computer telephone—talking over the Internet
- ★ Is your website customer friendly? Some tips

Chapter Twelve

Lights, Camera, Action: Service Stars

Most of you reading this book share at least one thing in common. You are not only service providers, you are service receivers. You come in contact with thousands upon thousands of customer service providers. In fact, I can think of no profession (and customer service is a profession) for which we should be better prepared through personal experience to do a great job.

Let's face it, we have seen it all: rude, indifferent, and exceptional care. We know what kind of service we like as well as the service that drives us crazy. Think of your personal experiences as a customer over the past week. Think of the best experience you had with a service

provider. Why was the experience special? My experience occurred upon arriving home from vacation. Since I was to be gone for ten days, I had decided not to leave my car at the airport and to take a taxi home. Upon arriving at 11:00 P.M. and getting my bags, I was assigned to a cab (actually a van) driven by Maurice. I was tired after the long flight but I was anxious to catch up on what had been going on at home while I was away. I was in luck! Maurice was friendly, talkative (not rambling), and genuinely anxious to engage in small talk. He quickly picked up on the fact that I was a local, and filled me in on how the weather had been, events going on in the city, and even the latest on local political races in progress. Had I been a tourist, I'm sure he was prepared with restaurant recommendations, sightseeing tips, and other useful information. When he dropped me off at home after midnight, he noticed that another passenger had left a bag in the backseat of the van. Remembering the passenger's address from the earlier drop-off, Maurice said, "Guess I'll stop by and deliver this bag on my way home. Mr. Jones (he remembered the passenger's name!) will need it in the morning." Now, Maurice may never be mayor or president of the chamber of commerce, but I can think of no one better suited to represent his city.

Maurice is a customer Service Star. There are hundreds of thousands of stars out there, but we need millions more! All of us can be stars. There are some very specific things we can do that will help us become a Service Star. And we can help our team be viewed as a real service-oriented team that stands out from other organizations and other businesses.

Let's first look at Service Stars. You all have them in your organizations. What they have in common is an intense desire to exceed the customer's expectations. They want their customers to walk away dazzled. Stars give everyone else goals to shoot for and a benchmark to be measured against. It's important to remember that everyone can become a star just by taking on the challenge of being exceptional.

Characteristics of a Service Star

- Motivation
- Flexibility
- Energy and enthusiasm
- Ownership

Motivated to Serve

All Service Stars share motivation—actually a passion—to serve and help others. Stars realize great personal satisfaction and reward from serving. They feel a genuine (and that word is important) need, want, and desire to help others.

Mario is an assistant general manager in one of the restaurants at the Pierre Hotel in New York City. Every day, he commutes to work, and that's enough to start anyone's day off on a low note. Well, Mario loves his job. He says that when he arrives at the restaurant and starts seeing the list of who's coming in for the day, and who they will be serving at this five-star hotel and restaurant, it's like caffeine starting to surge through him. He immediately gets excited about the day and getting ready to serve people.

Flexibility

In Chapter Nine we talked about all the different customers you have to deal with on a day-to-day basis, including the challenging ones. Flexibility is the key to being able to maneuver through all the craziness, all the customer demands, and all the challenges that get thrown at you every day. Customer Service Stars seem to be able to rise above negative situations and adapt their behavior based on the events going on around them.

Former *Good Morning America* co-anchor Joan Lunden had this to say in an interview shortly after learning she was to be replaced on the show. "I can admit to feeling scared and vulnerable sometimes. But then I talk to myself about how I choose to look at things. When life tosses you a curve ball, you can get mad, and say, 'Why did this happen to me?' or, 'Cool. Wonder if I can catch that ball.'" That's flexibility. We sometimes refer to it as making lemonade out of lemons. Service Stars know that recipe well and are flexible and adaptive enough to make gallons of lemonade every day on the frontlines of service.

Energy and Enthusiasm

Think about people you like to be around. They may be family members, friends, coworkers, or customers. No matter who they are, they are just plain fun to be around. They seem to radiate energy and enthusiasm. If you are having a bad day or are down in the dumps, just being around these people gives you a shot in the arm. Imagine the impact you could have on your customers by radiating energy and enthusiasm. Put another way, if you don't have energy and enthusiasm, change your mind and get it!

Ownership

Have you ever dealt with someone in an organization and come away feeling like you just talked to the president instead of a frontline associate? Have you ever said to yourself following a customer service interaction, "Gosh, I was lucky to get that person? I hope to get him or her again"? Or, "Wow! I can't believe they were able to do that for me." If you answered yes to these questions, you were lucky enough to be dealing with a real-life Service Star!

Service Stars take ownership of customers, situations, and problems. They use every bit of the power and authority they have been given by management. They make you feel like you are the only customer they have helped all day, even though they may have seen hundreds before you. Empowerment is a word that's a bit overused. But the meaning behind it is very powerful, especially as it relates to customer care. Stars take the power that they have been given to serve customers and to take ownership of their problems. In fact, true Service Stars find ways to help customers even when the letter of the law or policy prevents it.

Late one evening at a nursing home in the Chicago area, a senior manager decided to walk the floors a little to get some exercise. She encountered a young college student who worked part-time cleaning floors and doing other custodial tasks. Noticing how quiet it was that late at night, she told the young man that it would be fine if he brought in an iPod and listened to music to break the silence a little. Without hesitating, the young man replied, "Oh no, I couldn't do that. If one of the residents cried out or needed something, I wouldn't hear them." Talk about ownership! Here's a college student on a part-time job cleaning floors at night and he feels ownership for the care of the patients. Is he a Service Star? You bet.

Great Service Is HABITual

What daily habits can we engage in to help keep us motivated, energetic, enthusiastic, flexible, and empowered? These characteristics are states of mind. It's one thing to get up in the morning, look in the mirror, and say, "I think I'll be motivated at work today." It's another thing to follow through. Remember, exceptional customer service requires behavior modification. That means changing habits, practicing new techniques, and undoing some old ones. Here are a few for your consideration.

Be Consistent

Service Stars are consistent in how they deliver service. Have you ever purchased a new car? The day you first go to the dealership to look at cars the sales associate couldn't be nicer, more accommodating, willing to move heaven and earth to ensure you find just the automobile you want at a price you can afford. He's your best friend for that period of time. A week after you buy the car something minor needs adjusting, so you call the dealership. "Bill who? Oh yeah, why don't you call the service department and make an appointment to bring it in?" says the sales associate. I have no quarrel with having to call and schedule the car for service. I realize that the associate who sold me the car isn't the person who can fix it. It's just that I would like to feel a little of the charm, care, and concern that I experienced when I purchased the car carry over to at least my first service experience.

Contrast that with the philosophy of a local men's clothing store, where each customer is viewed as a lifetime customer. When patrons return to pick up an altered suit or trousers, associates go out of their way to treat them as well, or even better, than they did when they sold them the clothing. Service Stars have a way of making you feel special even after they have closed the deal.

Be Creative

There was a furniture store in Boston owned by two of the most creative and customer-oriented gentlemen we've met. These guys were not only Service Stars, they were borderline goofballs. They did all of their own television commercials (they were hilarious) and genuinely wanted to make furniture shopping fun. Here's where creativity comes in. These owners figured out that many customers bring small children with them. They also figured out that adults will stay longer and shop more seriously if the kids are happy. So they constructed a large children's play area inside the store with every type of game imaginable. By the way, you have to walk all the way through the store to get to the playground, so Mom and Dad can see the furniture before settling down to serious shopping. The kids are happy, so the parents are happy. It's simple. And one more thing. When you left their store, your car windows had been washed!

Creativity pays off both in terms of service and profitability. At a paper processing facility in eastern Tennessee, the associates in the shipping department had a group picture made of themselves. Every time a shipment of huge rolls of paper goes out, the people who prepared it for shipment circle their faces on the picture, sign their names, and enclose the picture with the shipment. What a creative way to take ownership and personalize an impersonal process like shipping paper!

Love What You Do

Motivation Factors as Rated by Employees*

1. Respect for my immediate supervisor
2. Feeling part of the organization
3. Comfort with the organizational culture
4. Meaningful work
5. Respect for senior leadership
6. Ability to learn and grow in the job
7. Benefits
8. Pay

*Engaging the Hourly Workforce, Corporate Executive Board Survey, October 2006

In almost every survey of the factors that motivate employees in the workplace, satisfaction with the job and "my boss" is at or near the top of the list, far surpassing pay and benefits. Service Stars, however, are far more than satisfied with their job and love what they do. If you have a frontline service job, you'd better love serving customers because you will be doing it eight or more hours a day. And customers can see straight through you and tell whether you enjoy your work.

I recently met a customer care associate who loves serving her customers. She works as a branch office administrator for Edward Jones, an international brokerage firm. Her office is in Daytona Beach, Florida. During the fires that damaged Florida from Jacksonville to Orlando, she went through her client list and made phone calls to customers who lived in the fire area simply to say, "How are you doing? Things okay? Do you need anything? Can we offer you a ride anywhere? Do you need some bottled water? Can we bring bottles to your house?" That only comes from somebody who loves her customers.

Pay Attention to the Details

There's a popular phrase, "Don't sweat the small stuff." While this might be good advice in dealing with stress in our personal lives, it doesn't apply in customer care. To customers, some more than others, everything is big stuff. If I work in a hospital and order flat sheets, I don't want to receive fitted sheets from the vendor. If I'm really particular about what kind of rental car I drive, I am concerned about that detail when I show up at the airport desk to claim my reserved car. Service Stars are very attentive to detail and go to great lengths to ensure that every need of their customer, however small, is met.

Nordstrom is well known in the retailing world for their great customer service. They started out many years ago as only a shoe store. The first time a customer comes in, they measure her feet. Not just one but both! When's the last time you had your feet measured prior to buying a pair of shoes? Just another detail that Star organizations attend to.

Love Change, Chaos, and Surprise

The world around us is changing so fast—technology, specific customer likes and dislikes, or the attitudes of society in general—that it hardly seems we have much choice but to embrace change. Service Stars thrive on change and the excitement and new opportunities that change creates.

Recharge Yourself

We talked about this earlier but it bears repeating. It is a rare individual who can stay motivated, energetic, and enthusiastic eight or more hours a day. We all need a break. Service Stars know when the stress, frustration, and workload is starting to get to them and that they need to take a break, to get offstage for a few minutes. These same individuals strive to maintain balance in their lives between work, family, and leisure activities.

Rate Your Service Star Habits

Which of the habits of Service Stars are you good at? Which do you need to improve on? Give yourself a grade from A (I'm a star at this) to F (I'm totally lacking in this habit).

Grade

Be consistent_____

Be creative _____

Love what you do _____

Pay attention to details _____

Love change, chaos, and surprise _____

Recharge yourself _____

Building Career Paths
Through Customer Care

Another characteristic of many Service Stars is a desire to be the best in their field, to excel in the profession of customer care. They know they are good at what they do and that they have top people skills. Perhaps they want to lead their customer service team or serve as a coach or a mentor to new associates.

With the growing trend in this country toward flatter organization structures, lateral moves and job shifts are becoming much more common. More than ever before, your ability to advance in the organization will be based on the value you add and the value you are able to create for your customers. According to the national executive recruiting firm, Korn-Ferry, "In the new millennium, people who will be rising to the senior ranks as presidents and CEOs will be those who understand customer value more so than at any time in the past."

How do you put yourself in the position to be recognized as someone who can take advantage of opportunities to move up in the organization? Here are some suggestions:

Better . . . Best

What might be exceptional service today will in all probability be just satisfactory service tomorrow. The bar is constantly being raised. Service Stars, in particular team leaders and coaches, are constantly asking the question, "How can I be 1 percent better at providing exceptional customer service today than I was yesterday?" Notice, I said 1 percent. Doesn't seem like much, but small, incremental improvements on a frequent basis are easier to achieve than large, breakthrough improvements. The now commonplace automated teller machine was a breakthrough service improvement in the financial services industry when it was invented in the 1960s. Since that time, numerous incremental improvements have been made in ATM technology, including range of services, accessibility, and security. Continuous improvement may come in attitude, communication, technology, or any of the areas we have discussed in this book. The important thing is constant improvement.

In his book, *Escape from the Box: The Wonder of Human Potential,* retired Air Force Colonel Edward Hubbard recounts his six and a half years as a prisoner of war during the Vietnam War. Hubbard reflects on the vast number of hours of spare time available to him and how he reviewed over and over every event of his then twenty-eight-year life that he could recall. In every case, he was able to think of ways he could have done better with just a tiny bit more effort. I think that is true of our customer service experiences as well. No matter how exceptional we are, there is always room for a 1 percent improvement.

The following exercise is designed to help you focus on small, incremental improvements to your service attitude and technique. You'll be surprised at how quickly these 1 percent improvements add up.

The time needed to complete this exercise is twenty minutes.

Exercise: The One Percent Solution

Instructions: Reflect on your last five encounters with customers (in person or over the telephone). Think through how you handled each situation, then try and identify and write down something you could have done to improve your response by 1 percent.

Customer Situation	1 Percent Improvement
1. Encountered a customer unhappy with the amount of his gas and electric bill.	I could have shown more empathy since everyone's bills are running high due to the extreme winter.
2.	
3.	
4.	
5.	

Look for Trends

Service Stars also watch for trends. If four customers complain about something in a short period of time, there may be a problem or a process that needs to be fixed. Look for trends and report them to your coach, manager, or leader. Information, or data, is one of the most valuable tools available to an organization. In Chapter 11, we talked about feedback and how we should beg for it. Feedback is a form of data. The late W. Edwards Deming had a favorite saying: "In God we trust, all others bring data." In business and industry, the entire basis of quality improvement is data-based decision making (rather than hunches and intuition). You can apply the same philosophy as you seek to constantly improve the quality of your service.

Here are a few examples of discovering trends:

- An office assistant notices an increase in erroneous shipments from a particular office supply company and reports it to the purchasing department.
- A nurse in the outpatient surgery department of a hospital notes an increase in telephone inquiries from patients about post-surgery wound care. Upon analyzing this data, the nurse discovers that the after-care information sheet sent home with patients is incomplete and needs to be revised.
- A mechanic in the service department of a car dealership performs a large number of repairs to the transmission on a particular new car model. He reports the problem to management, which in turn notifies the manufacturer in time to make modifications on the assembly line.

In each of these cases, the frontline associate could easily have ignored the data and continued to deal with the problems (incorrect supplies, more patient phone calls, higher number of car repairs). The mark of a Service Star is that they notice the trend and tell someone about it.

Take Initiative

While at a conference in Philadelphia recently, I stayed at a nice downtown hotel. Each morning, as I walked through the lobby, I noticed that the bellman had a stack of towels and a supply of water bottles sitting on his counter. After a couple of days, I asked him what the towels and water were for. He informed me that he has a lot of hotel guests who jog early in the morning, and they appreciate having a towel waiting for them upon their return, as well as a drink of water. Impressed with his creativity and innovation, I asked what made him start offering this service. He replied, "I thought to myself, what else can I do to make the early morning run more enjoyable for my customers?" No one told him to put towels and water out. He simply took the initiative because he knew it would make a positive impact on customer service. That's what Service Stars do.

Be Curious

Curiosity is another characteristic of associates creating customer value while advancing in their organizations. Service Stars have an almost unstoppable sense of curiosity. They know their organization inside and out. They keep up-to-date on new products, new processes, and new policies. Rarely do they have to tell a customer, "I don't know, but I'll find out." They have made it their business to anticipate customer questions and find out the answers in advance. The more progressive, forward-thinking companies in this country ensure that associates are continually exposed to all aspects of the business, both during initial orientation and then periodically. Salespeople should work on the production line; inventory control clerks should take a turn in the warehouse; customer service representatives should spend some time on the shipping floor; managers should work everywhere. And if your organization doesn't have a program for this, seek out the opportunity. Think to yourself for a moment, "What department or branch in the organization do I know the least about or would I like to know more about?" Then just say, "I'm curious."

You and Your Team

In this section we want to provide some specific suggestions for things you can do at team meetings to build a stronger team and ensure that everyone is really working together to provide exceptional customer service.

Team Tips

- Offer encouragement
- Brainstorm solutions
- Learn as a team
- Discuss new policies and procedures
- Identify areas for improvement

Offer Encouragement

Customer care is a day-in, day-out profession. Sometimes it can be a grind. Stress and burnout are always a danger. Perhaps the most valuable thing you can do as team members is offer encouragement to one another, particularly during stressful periods. Let your coworkers know that you empathize with their feelings. Maybe one of them has just encountered a nasty customer and is ready to walk. Perhaps it's been a day of frustrating situations, constant lines, or telephone queues that wouldn't stop. Talk with each other, give encouragement, but by all means stay positive. Don't engage in gripe sessions that will drag down the entire team.

Brainstorm Solutions

From time to time you will encounter customer problems with no obvious solution or challenging situations you haven't been confronted with before. Rather than spinning your wheels endlessly trying to find a solution, bring the problem or situation to a team meeting. Lay out the facts and ask for your team members' input. How would they handle the problem or situation? Someone may have been through the same situation recently and come up with a brilliant solution or phrase you can write down or post to use next time it comes up.

Team meetings should foster an environment in which it is okay to walk in and say, "Oh, I didn't do very well handling Mrs. Jones yesterday. Let me tell you how I messed up." Explain how you handled the situation and ask for input from team members on how you could have done better. This is a difficult thing to do because your ego is involved and it takes self-confidence to expose our shortcomings, especially to fellow team members. Experience is the best teacher, however, and you can learn and grow from your mistakes by letting others help. By the same token, don't be shy about parading a few successes out to the team. "Let me tell you what I did. It was so rewarding, and it worked! The customer loved it, and even sent me this letter saying so!" Again, there is a danger that you may come across as a braggart, but not if an environment has been set that encourages discussion of both failures and successes.

Team Learning

Another great idea is to set aside ten to fifteen minutes of every team meeting to learn something new. Maybe someone has a novel idea on how to handle a particular type of customer. Maybe someone has read an interesting article on some aspect of service that is worthy of sharing with the group. I recently stayed at the Marriott Hotel in New Orleans for a week and was impressed not only with the service but with the attitude and sense of teamwork of the staff. I asked several associates how they maintained that sense of unity and positive feeling toward customers. One of the first things they mentioned was the daily team meeting held early each morning. In addition to reviewing conventions and meetings currently in-house, as well as staffing assignments, the team takes time to discuss one of the Marriott "basics of the day." The day I inquired they were discussing "The Spirit to Serve," which they define as practicing teamwork and treating each other with the same respect they afford to their family and best customers. Their motto for the day was, "If we take care of each other, we will be able to take better care of our guests." Starting the day with some team training and discussion of core values can't help but put associates into the right customer care-oriented frame of mind.

Discuss New Policies and Procedures

Ho, hum! "Here's a new policy," says the team leader. "We need to discuss it this morning." Here's a different twist, however. Instead of just listening to and trying to understand the new policy or procedure, discuss as a team how best to explain the new policy to the customer. If the billing cycle is being changed, for example, anticipate customer reactions, particularly objections they might have, and figure out together how best to make them understand. If prices or fees are going up on certain products or services, anticipate customers' reactions and how you will convince them that they are still getting great value for their money.

Identify Areas for Improvement

You are the ones on the frontlines with the customers. You hear what they like, what they dislike, and what they think ought to be changed. In other words, take the verbal feedback you get from your customers on a daily basis and look at it critically. What changes could we make that might better serve the customer? Some of those changes might require management approval, while others can be implemented on the spot.

Remember, your customer service is only as strong as your team. Spending time together as a team, learning together, offering encouragement, and identifying areas for improvement, is time well spent because it gives you a chance to add value for your customers.

Remember: There Is No Silver Bullet

In this book we have talked about businesses from tire dealers to technological forerunners. From the doctor's office to the major call center, each business has its own set of challenges in creating the total customer experience. What is an after-the-service red rose on the car seat to one is a creative note or website to another.

What is important in today's highly competitive world is to do something, no matter how large or small, to improve customer service. Make your website customer friendly, greet patrons with a warm, genuine smile, listen carefully to feedback, be patient with upset customers, make sure you answer your voice mails promptly. The list goes on and on. A few require an investment of dollars or the approval of management to implement. Most require only self-approval and an investment of your time and energy. Again, the key is to do something. With so few doing much of anything to improve customer care, you'll be amazed at the difference you can make.

It's a Wrap

Did you catch all of the following points?

The Service Star: What does one look like?

- ★ Motivated to serve
- ★ Flexible
- ★ Energy and enthusiasm
- ★ Ownership

Great service is HABITual

- ★ Be consistent
- ★ Be creative
- ★ Love what you do
- ★ Pay attention to the details
- ★ Love change, chaos, and surprise
- ★ Recharge yourself

Moving up the customer service ladder

- ★ Be 1 percent better tomorrow than you are today
- ★ Watch for trends
- ★ Take the initiative
- ★ Be curious

Building a stronger service TEAM

- ★ Offer encouragement to each other
- ★ Brainstorm solutions to problems
- ★ Learn as a team
- ★ Discuss new policies and procedures
- ★ Identify improvement areas

Remember: There is no silver bullet

Index

Loving what you do, 189–90

Management
    cost of turnover in, 28
    empowering workers, 24, 32, 135, 187
    impacting customer care, 23
    team building, 196–98. *See also*
        Notes to team leaders, members, and management
Marriott Hotels, 24, 42, 198
Mission, remembering, 73–74, 77
Mistakes
    dealing with, 39, 55
    learning/growing from, 197
Moments of truth, 81, 83–84, 96
Money, customer service and, 74–75
Motivation, 185, 187, 189–90
Mystery shopping, 4, 73–74, 157, 159–62

Names
    badges with, 114
    giving and remembering, 113–14
    importance of, 107–8
    responding to callers by, 122–23
90/10 rule, 67, 77
Notes, taking, 100–101, 117, 125, 139
Notes to team leaders, members, and management
    books on positive thinking, 66
    cost of losing customer vs. cost of extra service, 26
    customer feedback issues, 150, 153, 167
    empowering solutions, 23
    evaluating constructive analysis, 35
    recognizing team members, 56
    recording phone conversations, 123
    recovering disappointed customers, 144

    shadowing program for associates, 196
    support system analysis and development, 62

One person, dealing with, 87, 92, 93, 96
Ownership, taking, 70–73, 77

Performance reviews, 29, 51, 53–54, 58. *See also* Self-assessment
Personal touch, 97–117. *See also* Communication; Listening
    changing times and, 104–5
    developing rapport, 106, 107–8
    ESEE (EASY) approach, 112–13
    eye contact and, 101–2, 111, 112
    giving and remembering names, 113–14
    hotel example, 108–9
    importance of, 98
    Listening to Yourself at Work exercise, 116
    losing, 97–98
    on phone. *See* Telephone skills
    summary points, 117
    10/5 rule, 111
    3 Cs and, 115
    using customer names, 107–8
    Zone of Influence and, 109–11
Pictures, communication and, 107
Plotting customer service. *See* Scattergram tool
Policies and procedures
    assessing, for exceptional service, 59
    charting customer process, 83
    new, discussing, 198
    policy stomping (not invoking "It's our policy."), 4, 140